COOL CAREERS WITHOUT COLLEGE FOR

PEOPLE
WHO LOVE
TO WRITE

COOL CAREERS WITHOUT COLLEGE FOR
PEOPLE
WHO LOVE
TO WRITE

GREG ROZA

The Rosen Publishing Group, Inc., New York

Published in 2007 by The Rosen Publishing Group, Inc.
29 East 21st Street, New York, NY 10010

First Edition

Library of Congress Cataloging-in-Publication Data

Roza, Greg.
Cool careers without college for people who love to write/
Greg Roza.
  p. cm.—(Cool careers without college)
Includes index.
ISBN 1-4042-0750-3 (library binding)
1. Authorship—Vocational guidance. I. Title. II. Series.
PN153.R69 2007
808'.02023—dc22

                                        2005031263

Manufactured in the United States of America

CONTENTS

INTRODUCTION

Our society is filled with careers for people who enjoy writing. There are probably more jobs out there than you think. Most positions require people to write persuasive letters, reports, summaries, and charts. People who excel at writing will have a colorful assortment of careers to pursue. The writing career you choose depends on the types of tasks you enjoy, your individual skills and talents, your level of experience, and the style of writing that you prefer.

Writers do more than sit in front of a computer screen waiting to think of believable dialogue or a catchy phrase. News reporters inform the public with their words; magazine writers educate and entertain; and copywriters use their words to persuade and sell. These are just three of the many careers available for people who enjoy writing. Some people are such effective writers that they work in more than one field. For example, many novelists work as book or magazine editors or copywriters during the day, while their nights and weekends are spent working out a tricky narrative. This may sound like a lot of work, but for the person who is truly passionate about writing and wants to do it professionally, it's just a typical day on the job.

While it might be true that some people have a natural talent for writing, anyone can become a writer in time if they work diligently enough. The information in this book is designed to help aspiring writers fully understand the variety of available job options available and the many ways in which they can achieve their goals. There are many character-building challenges ahead of you! This is just the first step to an exciting career as a writer.

1

NEWSPAPER REPORTER

You are on your way to the office of the local paper where you work one morning when you get a call from your managing editor. You have to rush downtown, where a congressman is giving an impromptu speech to his constituents about pollution issues in the state. Even though you have never met the man, it is your job to prepare questions, get an

News reporters, like the ones shown in this photograph of a CNN news-room in Atlanta, Georgia, often work in a large group. Although they each work independently, reporters sometimes consult their peers about various aspects of news reporting, such as developing a story's angle, maintaining objectivity, and writing engaging leads that hook readers.

interview, and report the facts. Timing is everything. Your job depends on getting the story quickly and making a good impression. Being a newspaper reporter can be an exciting and hectic job because you have to be ready for anything.

There are thousands of newspapers in the United States, all of them varying in size and scope. Whether they are serving big cities or small towns, all newspapers need reporters to investigate events and write about them every day. Depending on how big the company is, a newspaper may have hundreds of reporters or just a few.

Description

Newspaper reporters work with other editorial staff members—especially managing editors and copy editors—to investigate a topic or event and write about it. Reporters gather facts about various happenings, including community events, political developments, and crimes. Some reporters specialize in specific topics, such as sporting events or community meetings. Beat reporters often cover stories that occur in the same location—their beat—such as hospitals, schools, and courthouses. Most newspapers also depend on freelance writers and reporters who are commonly called stringers. Stringers investigate and report news events that occur in areas outside the local community or pursue less time-sensitive stories that "fill out" the paper when the news is slow.

Authoritative interviewing techniques and accurate note taking are two vital components of news reporting. Learning shorthand allows writers to take notes quickly. Although many reporters still use pen and paper when gathering the facts, some reporters use recorders to help them get the story. Others even carry cameras with them to take photos, or they may work closely with a professional photographer who is also assigned to the story.

Once reporters have completed their research, conducted interviews, and gathered as many facts as possible within a given period, they can begin writing an article.

Reporters might also use other resources, including reference materials, court documents, public records, and the Internet. Reporters must think and write objectively about their topics. It is important to report the facts of a story without allowing personal opinions to affect the angle of the article. Reporters often use a priority system to help them decide which facts are most important. In short, a reporter's main job is to write about situations or events in simple, precise language that the average reader can understand.

Reporters also have to meet daily or weekly deadlines. After a final proofing, reporters turn in their work to a senior or managing editor, who then reads the piece and often makes comments about it. The managing editor may or may not ask the reporter to change words or phrases. Sometimes, managing editors make those changes themselves.

Reporters must be able to work quickly and skillfully to meet recurring deadlines, which can sometimes be just a few hours after receiving an assignment. To meet these demands, some reporters relay their stories to editors over the phone or through e-mail.

News reporting is a demanding job. Busy newsrooms, challenging deadlines, frequent research, and dangerous assignments can cause a great deal of stress for any writer. If you like excitement and activity, however, writing for a newspaper might be the perfect job for you. The harder you

Journalism Terms

Byline The name of the writer appearing at the top of an article.

Caption Text that accompanies a photograph, illustration, graph, or chart.

Dateline A line of text at the beginning of an article that gives the time and location where the piece was written.

Feature An article of prominence in a newspaper.

Lead The first one to three paragraphs of a story.

Masthead The name and logo of the newspaper, which appear at the top of page 1. Sometimes called the flag or nameplate.

Sidebar Additional information that accompanies an article but is set apart from the regular text. This text is often placed in a box, and for this reason, sidebars are sometimes simply called boxes.

Tear sheet A page or several pages of a magazine or newspaper on which a writer's work is published.

This young intern researches a story for a Syracuse newspaper in upstate New York. Interns often research and write small items for daily and weekly newspapers such as classified ads, obituaries, and community calendars.

work, the more exciting your assignments will be—and the more pay you will receive.

Education and Training

Solid writing, communication, and typing skills are a must for reporters. Big-city newspapers—such as the *Chicago Tribune* and the *New York Times*—often hire only college graduates. However, newspapers serving small towns and local communities will hire a reporter based on his or her

News Agencies

A news agency is an organization supported by journalists with the intention of supplying breaking and continuous news reports to other news outlets, such as newspapers, television and radio news shows, and news-related Web sites. Most agencies supply a variety of media—including photographs, audio clips, and videotape footage—in addition to written news reports. A cooperative is a news agency that is owned and operated by the newspapers that contribute stories to it; these newspapers share the stories contributed to or written by the agency. Other news agencies are corporations that sell their news stories to other news venues. The Associated Press (AP) and Reuters are the two largest English-based news agencies in the world. AP is an American cooperative that claims to be the world's oldest and largest news agency. As of 2005, 1,700 newspapers and 5,000 television and radio outlets were members of AP. *The Associated Press Stylebook* has become the standard writing guide for American journalism. Reuters is a European news agency that sells news stories and financial information to news companies all over the world.

writing skills or past work experience. Personal qualities like curiosity, dedication, and determination are also extremely important. Small-town papers are more likely to hire someone straight out of high school than are newspapers serving a larger city or region. Many reporters gain experience and confidence at smaller papers and then move on to better positions in newspapers with greater circulations. Newspaper publishers consider past experience a valuable asset. Even working on your school newspaper or yearbook will help you gain the feel of a reporting career. Writing for television and radio news programs can also be useful.

Salary

Novice freelance or staff reporters can expect to make between $15,000 and $30,000 a year. More experienced reporters may make from $45,000 to $75,000 a year. Freelancers and stringers are paid based on what kind of articles they write and how long they are, the publication for which they write, and their level of experience.

Outlook

News reporting is a competitive field with many opportunities. Reporters usually work forty hours a week or more. Most are not compensated for overtime work. Many reporters spend nights and weekends reading or doing research to follow a story or to gain more insight on a topic.

News writers gain recognition with time by writing for larger publications that reach wider audiences. Some news writers have the potential to become newspaper editors, or managing editors.

FOR MORE INFORMATION

ORGANIZATIONS

Accuracy in Media (AIM)
4455 Connecticut Avenue NW
Suite 330
Washington, DC 20008
(202) 364-4401
Web site: http://www.aim.org

American Press Institute (API)
11690 Sunrise Valley Drive
Reston, VA 20191-1498
(703) 620-3611
Web site: http://www.americanpressinstitute.org

American Society of Journalists and Authors
1501 Broadway, Suite 302
New York, NY 10036
(212) 997-0947
Web site: http://www.asja.org

Fairness and Accuracy in Reporting (FAIR)
112 W. 27th Street

New York, NY 10001
(212) 633-6700
Web site: http://www.fair.org

First Amendment Center
Vanderbilt University
1207 18th Avenue S.
Nashville, TN 37212
(615) 727-1600
Web site: http://www.firstamendmentcenter.org

WEB SITES

Associated Press
http://www.ap.org
> One of the world's largest and most respected news organizations with offices around the world.

Detroit Free Press Jobs Page
http://www.freep.com/legacy/jobspaceindex.htm
> Articles, forums, and information for students interested in journalism careers.

Insert Text Here
http://www.inserttexthere.com
> A variety of resources for writers and reporters, including links, columns, job sites, and reference materials.

Journalism.org
http://www.journalism.org
> A valuable resource that incudes tips, tools, research, guidelines, and much more.

Newspaper Association of America
http://www.naa.org

A nonprofit organization that represents the newspaper industry. This site contains news and information about events, jobs, and trends in the field.

Reuters
http://today.reuters.com/news/default.aspx
The U.S. electronic edition of the international news agency.

United Press International
http://about.upi.com
A leading provider of information to news media outlets around the world.

BOOKS

Cappon, Rene J. *Associated Press Guide to News Writing: The Resource for Professional Journalists*. Lawrenceville, NJ: ARCO, 2000.

Cook, Bruce, and Harold Martin. *UPI Stylebook and Guide to Newswriting*. Sterling, VA: Capital Books, 2004.

Goldstein, Norm. *The Associated Press Stylebook and Briefing on Media Law*. New York, NY: Basic Books, 2004.

Harper, Timothy, ed. *The ASJA Guide to Freelance Writing: A Professional Guide to the Business for Nonfiction Writers of All Experience Levels*. New York, NY: American Society of Journalists and Authors, 2003.

Knight, Robert M. *A Journalistic Approach to Good Writing: The Craft of Clarity*. Ames, IA: Iowa State Press, 2003.

Kovach, Bill, and Tom Rosenstiel. *The Elements of Journalism: What Newspeople Should Know and the Public Should Expect*. New York, NY: Three Rivers Press, 2001.

Yudkin, Marcia. *Freelance Writing for Magazines and Newspapers: Breaking In Without Selling Out*. New York, NY: Harper & Row Publishers, 1988.

PERIODICALS

American Journalism Review (AJR)

University of Maryland
1117 Journalism Building
College Park, MD 20742-7111
(800) 827-0771
Web site: http://www.ajr.org

> *American Journalism Review* is a national publication that covers all aspects of print, television, radio, and online media.

Columbia Journalism Review

2950 Broadway
Columbia University
New York, NY 10027
(212) 854-1881
Web site: http://www.cjr.org

> *Columbia Journalism Review* is America's premier media monitor and watchdog publication. It was founded by the Columbia University School of Journalism.

Editor & Publisher

770 Broadway
New York, NY 10003-9595
(800) 641-2030
Web site: http://www.editorandpublisher.com

> *Editor & Publisher* is a leading trade publication of the newspaper industry with inside information on business, technology, electronic news reporting, and syndicates.

2

MAGAZINE WRITER

Compared to newswriting, magazine writing usually allows an author to write in a more individual and stylistic tone that reflects his or her own personal point of view. Magazine articles include interviews, book and film reviews, first-person accounts, essays, and more. Some magazines also publish short works of fiction or excerpts

Hendrick Hertzberg, political writer for the *New Yorker,* poses in his New York office in 2004. Political writers face the duel challenge of maintaining their objectivity while trying to impart a specific slant to feature articles and columns. Depending on the magazine, writers sometimes take an approach that leans toward the general opinions of their readership.

from fiction and nonfiction books. Many national and regional magazines accept dozens of freelance articles from writers every month. This demand for well-crafted articles provides plenty of opportunities for writers.

Description

Magazine writers create the articles that fill the pages of periodicals. Some are in-house staffers who work for a single publication, but many work on a contract or freelance basis for a variety of publications. Successful magazine writers stay busy throughout the year. The more articles they write, the higher their salaries. Publishing a variety of articles enables freelance writers to earn a solid reputation, which leads to more frequent assignments. Since they do not work under a supervisor's direction, freelance writers must remain focused on their schedules and deadlines.

Magazine writers new to the world of freelancing must be patient yet persistent when submitting their completed work or ideas for stories they would like to pursue. It may be weeks or months after submitting an article or query letter (a letter sent by a writer to an editor or publisher to pitch his or her idea for a proposed article) that a writer receives word from a publisher. Once a writer has had his or her first articles published, this process usually becomes more fruitful. Editors who have already accepted an article from a freelance writer are usually more receptive to future work by the same author. If a freelance writer works hard enough, he or she may even secure a regular relationship with a magazine's editorial staff, often leading to more frequent and higher-paying projects.

One of the common mistakes freelance writers make is not becoming familiar with the publications to which they submit their work. By reading a magazine from cover to cover, writers can familiarize themselves with the types of articles it prints and the style in which its articles are normally written. Some magazine editors even recommend

The Query Letter: Selling Yourself

First impressions mean everything in publishing. Your first impression as a freelance writer is usually made in your query letter. Editors are very busy people, and they want to know that your work is worth their time. A good query letter should be a brief but solid introduction to you and your ideas for the publication in which you would like to publish your work. Several book and Internet sources listed at the end of this chapter provide detailed information about writing effective query letters. Here is a brief list of important points to remember:

- Query letters should never be more than one page.
- The first half of your letter should sell your article with a persuasive, concise description.
- The second half of your letter should sell you as a writer. Provide a brief list of the articles you have published and the magazines that have published them. If you have not yet been published, explain your experience with the topic of the article you are trying to sell.

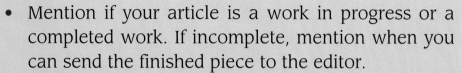

- Mention if your article is a work in progress or a completed work. If incomplete, mention when you can send the finished piece to the editor.
- Don't forget to include your contact information: name, address, phone numbers, and e-mail address.
- It is standard practice to include a self-addressed, stamped envelope (SASE) with your query letter so the editor can respond to you quickly and without having to pay for mailing supplies or postage.
- Proofread your query letter for spelling and grammar mistakes.

reading three issues of a magazine before submitting a proposal for any article. Successful freelance writers need to strive for a fresh, original approach to subject matter that is often repeated. The editors of specialized magazines, such as *Men's Health* and *Rock and Gem Magazine,* like to receive well-written articles that examine familiar topics in a new light. In addition, freelance writers need to follow a set of professional standards when submitting their work. In many cases, magazines set individual standards for submitted unsolicited articles. Follow these rules closely. If you don't, your work may not be considered, even if it is appropriate for publication. Check out the resources in the directory at

the end of this chapter for more information about things like proper manuscript format, effective query letters, and how to pitch ideas.

Education and Training

You do not need a college diploma to write magazine articles, though life experience is invaluable. Successful writers adore the written word, love crafting a well-written piece, and have a sincere desire to impart information to readers. The language and writing skills that you learn in high school are important for a career as a writer. Other extracurricular activities, such as writing for the yearbook or school newspaper, may also be useful. Practice editing your own work for spelling, grammar, and punctuation errors and then have an English teacher proofread it.

Continually educating yourself both inside and outside the classroom is vital to any writing career. Magazine writers often write about a wide variety of topics. Because of this, freelance writers need to be experts—or write like experts—about a great variety of topics. A mixture of good researching skills and effective writing habits will help you write articles that are both factual and engaging. Some writers, however, are actually experts on a particular subject. This requires learning all you can about the topic and staying up-to-date on developments in that field. After all, cutting-edge information often makes excellent content for the best magazine articles.

This young man is checking the contents of several books at his local library. In addition to gleaning information on the Internet, all writers should take the time to research and check facts in printed materials that relate to their subject matter.

Salary

Payment for an article is based on several criteria, such as length (often measured by the word count), expertise, and the publication. Well-known periodicals—such as *Atlantic Monthly* and the *New Yorker*—often pay as much as $1,000 to $2,000 per article, and sometimes more. Smaller publications offer much less compensation, perhaps between $10 and $300. Other publications offer only copies of the magazine as payment. Staff writers make between $20,000 and $65,000 a year and can establish lasting careers with single publications. Dedicated freelancers can make $20,000 a year or more, usually with a variety of publications. Some well-known freelancers make up to $500,000 a year.

Outlook

People read magazines at home, at work, in medical facilities, in hair salons, in gyms, and in many other public places. Supermarket shelves and newsstands are packed with magazines on hundreds of topics, from anthropology to zoology. If a freelance writer works hard enough, he or she can publish articles on a consistent basis. Some writers have full-time jobs and take freelance assignments on the side. Freelancing is a great way to supplement your income while building a name for yourself as a dependable writer.

FOR MORE INFORMATION

ORGANIZATIONS

Magazine Publishers of America (MPA)
810 7th Avenue, 24th Floor
New York, NY 10019
(212) 872-3700
Web site: http://www.magazine.org

WEB SITES

Freelance Writing Success
http://www.freelancewritingsuccess.com

This Web site contains dependable career advice for freelance writers.

Kid Magazine Writers
http://www.kidmagwriters.com
This is a unique source of information for children's magazine writers, including expert advice, detailed market information, and success stories.

Worldwide Freelance
http://www.worldwidefreelance.com
This Web site is loaded with tips on writers' markets and advice on selling your work and setting up a business.

Writing.com
http://www.writing.com
Another site that features a variety of useful resources.

BOOKS

Anderson Allen, Moira. *Starting Your Career as a Freelance Writer.* New York, NY: Allworth Press, 2003.

Anderson Allen, Moira. *Writer's Guide to Queries, Pitches, and Proposals.* New York, NY: Allworth Press, 2001.

Cook, Claire Kehrwald. *Line by Line: How to Edit Your Own Writing.* Boston, MA: Houghton Mifflin Company, 1985.

Cook, Claire Kehrwald. *2006 Writer's Market.* Cincinnati, OH: Writer's Digest Books, 2005.

Jacobi, Peter. *The Magazine Article: How to Think It, Plan It, Write It.* Bloomington, IN: Indiana University Press, 1997.

Johnson, Sammye, and Patricia Prijatel. *The Magazine from Cover to Cover: Inside a Dynamic Industry.* New York, NY: McGraw Hill, 1999.

Mandell, Judy. *Magazine Editors Talk to Writers.* New York, NY: John Wiley & Sons, 1996.

University of Chicago Press. *The Chicago Manual of Style.* 15th ed. Chicago, IL: University of Chicago Press, 2003.

Wray, Cheryl Sloan. *Writing for Magazines: A Beginner's Guide*. Lincolnwood, IL: NTC/Contemporary Publishing, 1996.

PERIODICALS

Folio
33 South Main Street
Norwalk, CT 06854
(203) 854-6730
Web site: http://www.foliomag.com
The industry leader of trade and consumer magazine publishers.

Writer
21027 Crossroads Circle
Waukesha, WI 53186
(262) 796-8776
Web site: http://www.writermag.com
This is a popular consumer magazine that features regular information about writing effective query letters, contacting publishers, and selling your written work.

Writer's Digest
4700 E. Galbraith Road
Cincinnati, OH 45236
(513) 531-2222
Web site: http://www.writersdigest.com
Each issue of *Writer's Digest* contains valuable information for all types of writers. Its companion Web site has an abundance of useful resources, including writing tips, market listings, and contest and workshop notifications.

3

COLUMNIST

People who write articles for newspapers must stick to the facts. Readers expect an objective and unbiased view of the subject matter, whether it is a local or international news story. However, every writer has his or her own opinion. If you are a writer who yearns to write from a personal point of view and offer your opinions rather than simply

Sports writer Sam Lacy poses at the *Afro American Newspaper* in Baltimore, Maryland. In 1948, Lacy was the first African American sports writer allowed into the Baseball Writers' Association.

report the facts, you may want to consider pursuing a career as a columnist.

Description

Columnists write daily, weekly, or monthly opinion pieces for newspapers, magazines, and electronic news sites. Political or news columns generally appear in the op-ed pages in a newspaper. Some columnists are even paid to read their columns on public radio stations or television news shows. Every columnist writes about something that interests him or her, whether that's sports, fashion, humor,

family life, or cooking. Many write about government and political activities. Others write advice columns about personal or motivational topics that follow a specific theme. Still others write humorous pieces about whatever crosses their minds when they sit down at their desks. The one thing all of these columnists have in common is that they are speaking their minds and not just reporting the facts.

Much like newspaper reporters, columnists are curious people who want to know more about many topics. Although columnists use their opinions and personalized writing style to shape their columns, much of their job relies heavily on research. Columnists must be careful to relate the facts of a story, like reporters do, before they express their opinions about it.

Columnists often read the news and listen to current events on both the television and radio to come up with ideas and hear public opinion. The columnist examines the news story or report and then uses his or her personal style to express an opinion about the subject matter. This often makes columns more exciting or interesting than news articles. Some columnists are masters of satire and parody, two writing devices that are never allowed in a news article.

Columnists usually follow a rigid schedule, and they must meet regular deadlines depending on how often the publication for which they write is printed—daily, weekly, monthly, or quarterly. Freelance columnists may work less frequently, but they must work consistently nonetheless in order to make a solid living. Many freelance columnists become full-time writers for newspapers or magazines after they have established a significant readership.

As a columnist, you will find that the larger your audience, the more publications will be interested in running your column on a regular basis. Popular columnists often become syndicated. This means that their columns are printed by more than one newspaper. Some columns are printed nationally by as many publications that want to run it. A syndicate is a marketing company that sells your work to as many publications as it can and then takes a portion of the profits earned by those sales. The more publications that print your column, the more money you earn.

Education and Training

A good way to start training for a career as a columnist is to write articles for your school newspaper. You might even start your own column. Joining a debate team will teach you how to effectively express your own opinions about a subject and may offer you some feedback on those opinions.

When training to become a columnist, it is important to read the work of other columnists. Read five or six columnists on a regular basis. Choose the work of a few who write about topics that interest you. Seek the work of other columnists for different reasons, perhaps simply because they are popular or because their opinions are different from your own.

How Is a Column or Editorial Different from a News Article?

Most newspapers and magazines print columns in every issue. But how is a column different from a regular news article? The most important difference is that columns are expressions of the author's opinion and not just a report of the facts. A column is generally shorter than a newspaper or magazine article—usually between 400 and 1,000 words. A column is short enough to be read quickly and long enough to entertain its readers with well-developed ideas. It usually has a catchy beginning, a concise but descriptive middle, and a strong ending that readers will remember.

An editorial is another kind of opinion piece. Editorials are generally written by the editorial board of a news organization and appear without bylines. An editorial is usually meant to express the collective opinion of the organization and not that of an individual. Editorials usually take up an entire page of the newspaper, and they are usually about current events. The op-ed page (which is literally opposite the editorial page) features letters to the editor from readers who want to express their own opinions about editorials or other matters.

This will help you become familiar with the basic structure of a column. It will also expose you to different writing styles and ways of thinking, which will help you to establish your own individual style and voice.

Salary

In general, columnists make more money than reporters. Some starting columnists can earn between $20,000 and $30,000 a year. More experienced columnists may earn between $60,000 and $100,000 or more. Freelance columnists normally get paid per column, and that amount depends on the individual publication. Syndicates usually take between 40 and 60 percent of the profit.

Outlook

Most columnists begin their careers as reporters or editors and work their way up to positions as columnists. Compared to news reporters, columnists must compete for far fewer positions, and former reporters usually secure most of them. Because of this, pursuing a career as a columnist is much

Carolyn Wyman, a nationally syndicated food columnist who has written a book entitled *The Kitchen Sink Cookbook: Offbeat Recipes from Unusual Ingredients*, poses in a clothes dryer with the results of one of her recipes: clothes dryer shrimp.

easier if you first work as a reporter. It is best to start at a newspaper with a small editorial staff. This will allow you the opportunity to move up quickly should a columnist position become available.

FOR MORE INFORMATION

ORGANIZATIONS

The American Society of Journalists and Authors (ASJA)
1501 Broadway, Suite 302
New York, NY 10036
(212) 997-0947
Web site: http://www.asja.org

The National Society of Newspaper Columnists (NSNC)
1345 Fillmore Street, Suite 507
San Francisco, CA 94115
(415) 563-5403
Web site: http://www.columnists.com

WEB SITES

Blue Eagle Commentary
http://blueagle.com/index.html
   This site includes information about American columnists.

Writing-World.com
http://www.writing-world.com/links/syndication.shtml
   This section of the Writing World Web site contains information about popular syndicates.

BOOKS

Anderson Allen, Moira. *Writer's Guide to Queries, Pitches, and Proposals*. New York, NY: Allworth Press, 2001.

Bly, Bob. *Become a Recognized Authority in Your Field in 60 Days or Less!* Indianapolis, IN: Alpha Books, 2002.

Digregorio, Charlotte. *You Can Be a Columnist: Writing and Selling Your Way to Prestige*. Portland, OR: Civetta Press, 1993.

Fink, Conrad C. *Writing Opinion for Impact*. Ames, IA: Blackwell Publishing, 2004.

McCabe-Cardoza, Monica. *You Can Write a Column*. Cincinnati, OH: Writer's Digest Books, 2000.

Sloan, William David, and Laird B. Anderson, eds. *Pulitzer Prize Editorials: America's Best Writing, 1917–2003*. Ames, IA: Iowa State University Press, 2003.

Taylor, David. *The Freelance Success Book: Insider Secrets for Selling Every Word You Write*. Savannah, GA: Peak Writing Press, 2003.

PERIODICALS

Byline
P.O. Box 5240
Edmond, OK 73083-5240
(405) 348-5591
Web site: http://www.bylinemag.com
Byline is a magazine that offers advice and feature articles about the business of freelance writing.

Poets & Writers
72 Spring Street, Suite 301
New York, NY 10012
(212) 226-3586
Web site: http://www.pw.org
Poets & Writers is a national magazine that offers information, support, and guidance for creative writers. It was founded in 1970 and is the nation's largest nonprofit literary organization.

4

CRITIC/ REVIEWER

Do you consider yourself a film or gadget buff? Do you love to read the latest books? Are you a music fanatic? Are you someone who enjoys dining at the latest restaurants? If you are a writer who enjoys music, films, plays, books, or fine dining, you might consider becoming a critic or reviewer. A critic is usually someone with a well-known and respected background in his or her field, while a reviewer could be a writer who is more of a generalist. Not only is writing about entertainment fun, it's a career with plenty of perks: free film and theater tickets; tons of CDs, DVDs, computer software, and demos; copies of books long before they are released to the public; and swarms of people rushing to bring you the finest fare they have to offer. Sound good? Read on.

Description

Critics and reviewers are experts in specific fields. Critics also write with style and authority. Knowledge of industry trends in categories such as the following are often necessary to become a critical reviewer: contemporary publishing, the music industry, theatrical entertainment and dance, film, fashion and retailing, restaurants and cooking, technology, and automobiles. You can be a freelance or a staff reviewer. Some critics' reviews are even syndicated.

Similar to columnists, critics and reviewers have strong opinions, though that isn't enough to excel in this profession. Readers are more likely to respect your opinions when you can offer a keen insight into how you formed them. Can you compare a band's new release to its earlier catalog of titles? How about the latest software? How is it better or worse than the company's earlier versions? Critics and reviewers rely on their extensive knowledge to back up

Retired *New Yorker* film critic Pauline Kael lectures from her home in Great Barrington, Massachusetts, where she wrote reviews and commuted to New York for film screenings. In 2001, Kael was named the inaugural recipient of Columbia University School of Journalism's Distinguished Lecturer in Criticism.

their opinions. It isn't enough to say that the new CD by the Dave Matthews Band is excellent or horrible. You must know enough about music, songwriting, and the music industry to explain why it is either a groundbreaking or a repeat performance.

In addition to individual expertise, both critics and reviewers need to develop effective writing skills and an authoritative and persuasive voice. As in any other writing career, publishers may turn down your review if it contains spelling errors, grammatical mistakes, or formatting problems.

Once you sell your first review, others will generally follow. Many freelancers use their first few reviews as a foundation for new publishing clients. Successful reviewers also often receive comps such as electronics, books, film and theater tickets, and CDs. These are giveaways from companies that are hoping for favorable press and the chance to obtain some free promotion in newspapers and magazines.

Sometimes critics must deal with hard feelings from readers. Some readers will agree with your opinions; others will not. On rare occasions, readers are offended when they read negative reviews about their favorite artists. As any critic will reveal, some readers respond to critics with unkind letters. Negative response is difficult to avoid when you are a critic.

Education and Training

While critics do not require a college degree, they do need to be experts in their chosen field. You can achieve this expertise through a combination of methods. First and most important, you need to immerse yourself in the area about which you want to write. If you want to be a reviewer of plays, for example, you need to attend as many theatrical performances as you can. If you like to follow trends in fashion, attend as many fashion shows as you can. In general, all potential critics should learn as much as possible about their chosen fields. Read books by experts. Watch related movies and

Work Environment

Critics and reviewers—regardless of their areas of expertise—must immerse themselves in their fields. If you are a critic of popular films, you must see just about every movie that appears in the theaters and perhaps also movies that go straight to DVD or video. Book reviewers read books constantly and quickly. Restaurant critics eat at different restaurants on a weekly or daily basis. Electronics reviewers continually purchase (or receive) electronic devices in order to test them and write related reviews.

In many respects, critics and reviewers are fortunate to be paid to do exactly what they like to do, whether that's dining out, reading new books, listening to new music, or seeing new films. Keep in mind, however, that unless you truly love the area you've chosen to work in, there is a chance that you may grow tired of doing one thing all the time. In short, make sure you love what you do before deciding to make it your career. Otherwise, you may "burn out," a phrase that is often applied to writers who have lost interest in writing and whose work has lost its impact.

Writer Eric Olsen works from his home on the Web site he created, Blogcritics.org, to offer critical reviews of book, music, and film releases. Olsen says that because the U.S. copyright laws prohibit tampering with copy-protection measures used on DVDs, he cannot offer sound bites or film trailers on his site, even for legally permitted "fair uses."

documentaries. Speak with established professionals. Attend workshops. Learn to anticipate trends. Above all, learn the history of the field in which you are offering your critical opinion.

To become more familiar with authoritative and persuasive writing styles, select four or five critics and read as many of their reviews as possible. Choose a few critics you like and a couple you dislike. Pay attention to the ideas on which all the reviews focus and the descriptive terms they use to describe those ideas. The knowledge you gain from reading published work will help you create your own individual writing style later.

Salary

The salary that you can make as a critic or reviewer is often similar to that of a columnist. Depending on the publication, freelance reviewers with slight experience may make as little as $25 a review. Other writers who have honed their skills and published reviews in a few magazines or newspapers may make $300 per review or more. A reviewer with a regular column could make $30,000, $40,000, or more.

Outlook

A career as a critic or reviewer is more specialized than a career as a news reporter, and the positions can be especially hard to come by because there are so few of them. Your success in this specialized writing field depends on your overall experience as a writer and your knowledge of what you are reviewing. Many reviewers and critics begin as freelance writers working for small-town papers. After a while, their editors may offer them a chance to write a review. They then can gain more experience and make the transition to larger newspapers and magazines. As with any writing career, determination, persistence, and a thick skin will help you succeed.

FOR MORE INFORMATION

ORGANIZATIONS

American Library Association
50 East Huron Street
Chicago, IL 60611
(800) 545-2433
Web site: http://www.ala.org

WEB SITES

All Music Guide
http://www.allmusic.com
> This is one of the most comprehensive music review sites on the Internet. It features thousands of reviews of every genre of music.

CNET.com
http://www.cnet.com
> This site is loaded with up-to-date facts and reviews to help consumers make informed choices about entertainment-related purchases.

Metacritic
http://www.metacritic.com
> This site features thousands of film, DVD, and video reviews.

The New York Times Theater Reviews
http://theater.nytimes.com/pages/theater/index.html
> A comprehensive look at well-written reviews of plays, musicals, dance, and performance pieces from New York City and around the world.

BOOKS

Carr, Jay, ed. *The A List: The National Society of Film Critics' 100 Essential Films.* Cambridge, MA: Da Capo Press, 2002.

Horning, Kathleen T. *From Cover to Cover: Evaluating and Reviewing Children's Books.* New York, NY: HarperCollins Publishers, 1997.

Hughes, Holly, ed. *Best Food Writing 2005.* New York, NY: Marlowe & Company, 2005.

Ross-Larson, Bruce. *Edit Yourself: A Manual for Everyone Who Works with Words.* New York, NY: W. W. Norton, 1996.

Steele, Valerie. *Fifty Years of Fashion: New Look to Now.* New Haven, CT: Yale University, 2000.

Trimble, John R. *Writing with Style: Conversations on the Art of Writing.* Upper Saddle River, NJ: Prentice Hall Press, 2000.

PERIODICALS

Booklist
The American Library Association
50 East Huron Street
Chicago, IL 60611
(800) 545-2433
Web site: http://www.ala.org/booklist
> This trade magazine about the book publishing industry is loaded with monthly book reviews from a variety of staff and freelance book critics.

Rolling Stone
1290 Avenue of the Americas
New York, NY 10104-0298
(212) 484-1616
Web site: http://www.rollingstone.com
> This well-known and long-standing music monthly features reviews of albums, singles, and DVDs.

NOVELIST

Are you a creative and imaginative person who enjoys telling stories? Do you write short stories and poems? If you are the type of person who can craft a believable story and who also has a knack for writing dialogue, then you may have what it takes to become a novelist. Becoming a novelist is among the most difficult challenges

New Hampshire author Dan Brown signs copies of his book *The Da Vinci Code* in 2003. The book, which went on to become a national best-seller, is a mixture of code breaking, art history, secret societies, religion, and lore, all wrapped up in a fast-paced thriller that unravels in a twenty-four-hour period.

for a writer. If you like writing, however, and don't mind the diligent, hard work required to develop characters and plots, then writing a novel can be satisfying and inspirational.

Description

Perhaps the most valuable trait a novelist can have is dedication. For every word in a novel, the author may have

written ten others that were revised. Practice is essential. You must write (and read) constantly, or, at the very least, regularly. Reading is an excellent way to improve as a writer.

A novelist's approach to his or her job is an individual one. Some novelists set aside a certain time of the day or week to write; others go at it in spurts. Some novelists treat writing as a full-time job. Others will write as little as two pages a day. At this rate, they would produce more than 700 pages of first-draft material in one year. Still, all writers revise their work, which can also be time-consuming. Some novelists revise once or twice, while others revise for years. Writing any novel takes a considerable amount of time. Most authors will work on a novel for a minimum of one to three years. The most important thing for a novelist is to establish a writing regimen and maintain it.

It is also important to research the novel market frequently and to stay on top of the latest news about the publishing industry. When a writer finishes a novel, he or she submits it to an agent or publisher. The manuscript must be typed and formatted according to industry standards and the specific guidelines of the publisher.

Education and Training

Some of our greatest writers never graduated from college: Louisa May Alcott, Ernest Hemingway, and James Baldwin, to name just a few. While a formal education can certainly help you develop any writing career, becoming a novelist is often more dependent on personality and a drive to succeed. You can start to develop many of the skills necessary to become a novelist in high school. Writers write about what they know and understand. Even fantasy and science fiction writers use experiences from their lives to create characters, plots, dialogue, and themes.

Writers always look for chances to learn new things. When asked by aspiring authors for advice, many established writers tell them to read as much as possible. Reading a variety of texts, from novels to newspaper articles, will strengthen your knowledge of vocabulary and grammar and educate you about a wide range of topics. You will also encounter an abundance of styles, which will help you find your own.

Salary

While it may be difficult to become a published novelist, publishing your first novel can be both emotionally and financially rewarding. You may sell your first novel for $10,000 to $50,000, and you may receive more money if the book does well or when the paperback edition is printed. In 2004, British novelist J. K. Rowling earned close to $200 million, making her the highest-paid novelist in history.

The National Book Awards fiction finalists autograph copies of their books in 2004 at a Barnes & Noble bookstore in New York City. From left are: Christine Schutt, author of *Florida*; Joan Silber, author of *Ideas of Heaven: A Ring of Stories*; Lily Tuck, author of *The News from Paraquay*; and Kate Walbert, author of *Our Kind: A Novel in Stories*.

Outlook

Once you've submitted your work to an agent or publisher, the waiting game begins. It can take months to receive a response from the publisher, or you may never receive one. Rejection letters are sure to pile up before you receive positive feedback, and a favorable response does not necessarily mean that your work will even be published. Many people yearn to establish a career as a novelist, but a mere fraction of those people achieve their dream.

Writing novels, however, is much like any other art form. Most artists don't think of their art as a way to earn money. Novelists write because they enjoy it. The best advice to an aspiring novelist is perhaps also the most difficult to hear: plan on establishing a career as a novelist while you earn money doing something else. Many novelists are also teachers, publishers, editors, newspaper reporters, and so on. These careers allow novelists to perfect their professional writing skills while also writing for pleasure.

FOR MORE INFORMATION

ORGANIZATIONS

The Author's Guild
31 E. 28th Street, 10th Floor
New York, NY 10016-7923
(212) 563-5904
Web site: http://www.authorsguild.org

Canadian Author's Association (CAA)
320 South Shores Road
P.O. Box 419

Campbellford, ON K0L 1L0
Canada
(705) 653-0323
Web site: http://www.canauthors.org

WEB SITES

Novelists, Inc.
http://www.ninc.com
> This Web site is mainly for published authors. It keeps members connected and well-informed about the fiction market.

Writers Market
http://www.writersmarket.com
> This site charges a fee, but it allows users to easily browse up-to-date market information and addresses of publishers and their individual editors.

Writing-World.com
http://www.writing-world.com/index.shtml
> This site contains a wealth of information for writers, including columns, how-tos, advice, and market information.

BOOKS

Anderson Allen, Moira. *Writer's Guide to Queries, Pitches, and Proposals*. New York, NY: Allworth Press, 2001.

Bowling, Anne, and Michael Schweer, eds. *2006 Novel and Short Story Writer's Market*. Cincinnati, OH: Writer's Digest Books, 2005.

Brande, Dorothea. *Becoming a Writer.* New York, NY: Penguin Putnam, 1981.

Brogan, Kathryn S., ed. *2005 Guide to Literary Agents*. Cincinnati, OH: Writer's Digest Books, 2004.

Gotham Writer's Workshop. *Writing Fiction: The Practical Guide from New York's Acclaimed Creative Writing School*. New York, NY: Bloomsbury, 2003.

Mandell, Judy. *Book Editors Talk to Writers*. New York, NY: John Wiley & Sons, 1995.

Merriam-Webster. *Merriam Webster's Manual for Writers and Editors*. Springfield, MA: Merriam-Webster, 1998.

PERIODICALS

Writer
21027 Crossroads Circle
Waukesha, WI 53186
(262) 796-8776
Web site: http://www.writermag.com
> This magazine offers plenty of writing resources, as well as information about conferences, forums, writing groups around the world, and features and advice columns.

Writer's Digest
4700 E. Galbraith Road
Cincinnati, OH 45236
(513) 531-2222
Web site: http://www.writersdigest.com
> This is the electronic companion to another leading print consumer magazine for writers. It features advice columns, ways to manage your writing career, ideas for new books and articles, and general reference information.

6

SCREENWRITER

The feature film and television industries are two of the biggest money-making fields in the world, and both require screenwriters. Writers are also needed to create scripts for educational films, promotional films, and newscasts. Working as a screenwriter can be exciting, but it is often a difficult career filled with stumbling blocks. Even

Finding Neverland producer Richard Gladstein *(second from left)* stands next to *Eternal Sunshine of the Spotless Mind* writer Charlie Kaufman *(second from right)* and *Million Dollar Baby* writer Paul Haggis *(right)* during industry panel discussions at the 20th Annual Santa Barbara International Film Festival in Santa Barbara, California, in 2005.

so, there are a few options available for those without a college education, but you must be an undying promoter of your work. Develop skills as a salesperson, and grow a thick skin while you're at it.

Description

Screenwriting is a demanding career. Once a writer completes a screenplay, he or she needs to sell it. Producers are

notoriously demanding, and working with them can be frustrating. Although screenwriters may not need agents to sell their work to smaller production companies, they definitely need agents when dealing with large Hollywood or New York studios.

Script readers want fresh scripts. The writer needs to find a way to breathe new life into old themes. Agents and editors are also looking for colorful characters, highly visual elements that will look spectacular on film, and a hook—an idea that will capture the audience's attention. These elements make screenplays more popular and therefore more profitable.

Some screenwriters begin their careers by writing and producing short films (shorts) or independent films (indies). If you are able to write a short narrative, this is a great way to develop your screenwriting skills and learn the ropes of the filmmaking industry. Keep in mind, however, that you need to find funding for these two options. This usually means that you will need the help of others who are also hoping to break in to the moviemaking industry.

Many writers publish their stories or novels before thinking of adapting them into screenplays. Having a novel accepted for publication shows agents and editors that it might make a good film or television script. (Most production companies now prefer to adapt previously written works and use preexisting stories as a way to save money.)

Some experts in the film industry agree that the most important part of a screenplay is the first ten to fifteen pages.

What Is a Pitch?

The pitch is a vital step for all screenwriters. Pitching a script means selling it verbally to a producer. Pitching your story is more like acting than writing. Here is a list of tips to help you pitch with the best of them.

- Don't just wing it. Some screenwriters are so confident in their speaking abilities that they think the perfect pitch will simply come to them. Many of these people end up losing an opportunity to sell their screenplay because their pitch falls flat. Practice pitching your screenplay to another screenwriter.
- Your pitch should be somewhat detailed but to the point. Aim for a ten-minute plot synopsis.
- Your pitch should focus on a single character. Think of this character as the "star" of your screenplay. Emphasize the traits that will make an actor want to play that character in a movie.
- Unravel the story about the main character. What happens to him or her? What problems does he or she face? What are the results of his or her struggle?

- Producers need to know how to market your ideas. Emphasize the genre, or category, of movie that you have written. Point out the type of audience who would want to see it.
- Emphasize the qualities that will make a director want to turn your screenplay into a movie. Directors seek strong stories with unique characters.

This is the information that will either grab a reader's attention or cause him or her to toss your story aside. Once you've gotten your reader's attention, you need to develop the action of the story. Other experts will tell you that the last ten pages are just as crucial as the first ten pages. Drawing readers into a closing climax scene is as important as concluding your ideas without leaving crucial questions unanswered. More than anything, the story should feel complete, with a beginning, middle, and end.

Education and Training

Although watching movies may not seem educational, it will help to improve your storytelling technique. Reading screenplays written by other writers may also help you develop your ideas. (Some resources for finding screenplays are provided at the end of this chapter.) At the very least, reading

Television writer Janis Hirsch poses at her home in Los Angeles, California. When Hirsch heard that a former writer's assistant for the TV show *Friends* had filed a sexual harassment lawsuit over crass jokes and comments made by male writers, sympathy wasn't her first reaction. According to Hirsch, anything goes when writers get together to discuss scripts, dialogue, story arcs, and plotlines.

screenplays will show you the proper format for a screenplay, without which you simply won't sell your work. It may help to watch a movie while reading the script at the same time.

You should also try to familiarize yourself with the film and television industry by reading trade magazines, going to film festivals, and participating in screenwriting contests.

Salary

It may take years for you to earn a salary as a screenwriter, and the range of salaries in the industry is huge. You may make nothing, especially when working on independent films. Well-known, successful screenwriters can make millions on a single script, in addition to a percentage of what the finished film takes in as profit. Staff screenwriters usually earn salaries ranging from $30,000 to $85,000 a year.

Screenplay Terms

Logline One or two sentences at the beginning of a treatment that is designed to grab the reader's attention. Loglines are also used in face-to-face meetings between writers and producers.

Query letter As with novelists and magazine writers, screenwriters often sell their screenplays or ideas for screenplays by sending out well-crafted query letters. The query letter is usually the first contact between a writer and the person or persons who will buy his or her screenplay.

Step outline A screenplay summary that includes one sentence for each scene. Some studios expect to see a step outline before accepting a screenplay.

Synopsis A one-page summary of the plot of your screenplay. The synopsis is an important tool when pitching your work.

Treatment A scene-by-scene summary of the screenplay without dialogue. Treatments are usually about thirty to fifty pages long and include a logline and a one-to-three page synopsis that describes the events and characters. Writers are often paid a portion of their fee upon submitting their treatment to an editor.

Outlook

The screenwriting business is competitive, even more so than careers in book or magazine publishing. It costs far more to make a film than it does to publish a novel. Think of all the people who work on a movie set: actors, directors, writers, camera people, fashion experts, stylists, and many others. Because of their large budgets, movie producers often want to work with established screenwriters who have already written profitable screenplays.

This is not to say that screenwriting isn't worth your time or that you cannot succeed in this field. It does mean that you will have to work hard and remain determined, even as the rejection letters pile up. Learn what you can from these rejections, and master the rules for preparing and submitting your screenplay as your writing improves. Your chances of selling your script will increase as you build a reputation as a dependable, capable writer.

FOR MORE INFORMATION

ORGANIZATIONS

American Screenwriters Association
269 S. Beverly Drive, Suite 2600
Beverly Hills, CA 90212-3807
(866) 265-9091
Web site: http://www.asascreenwriters.com

Screenwriters Guild of America
4337 Marina City Drive, Suite 1141
Marina del Rey, CA 90292
Web site: http://screenwritersguild.org

WEB SITES

Red Inkworks
http://www.redinkworks.com
    This Web site features information about screenplay formatting.

Screenwriters Online
http://www.screenwriter.com
    This Web site is a forum for professional screenwriters that offers
    valuable services, including script reading and workshops.

Screenwriter's Web: Script Marketing Advice
http://www.breakingin.net
    Plentiful information can be found at this Web site, including
    advice from experts, tutorials, and much more.

Simply Scripts
http://www.simplyscripts.com
> This site offers hundreds of free screenplays for writers learning the genre.

BOOKS

Breimer, Stephen. *The Screenwriter's Legal Guide*. New York, NY: Allworth Press, 2004.

Engle, Joel. *Oscar-Winning Screenwriters on Screenwriting: The Award-Winning Best in the Business Discuss Their Craft.* New York, NY: Hyperion, 2002.

Iglesias, Karl. *The 101 Habits of Highly Successful Screenwriters: Insider's Secrets from Hollywood's Top Writers*. Cincinnati, OH: Adams Media Corporation, 2001.

Seger, Linda. *Making a Good Script Great.* Hollywood, CA: Samuel French Trade, 1994.

Trottier, David. *The Screenwriter's Bible: A Complete Guide to Writing, Formatting, and Selling Your Script*. Los Angeles, CA: Silman-James Press, 1998.

PERIODICALS

Canadian Screenwriter
Writer's Guild of Canada
366 Adelaide Street West, Suite 401
Toronto, ON MSV 1R9
Canada
Web site: http://www.wga.ca/magazine/index.html
> This is a quarterly publication that has been serving Canadian screenwriters since 1998.

Creative Screenwriting
6404 Hollywood Boulevard, Suite 415
Los Angeles, CA 90028

(800) 727-6978

Web site: http://www.creativescreenwriting.com

This magazine features news about recent or soon-to-be-released films and their screenplays.

Hollywood Scriptwriter

P.O. Box 11163

Carson, CA 90746

(310) 530-0000

Web site: http://www.hollywoodscriptwriter.com

Another trade publication that includes insider information and updates about movers and shakers in the industry and their projects.

ScreenTalk

2500 New Brighton Boulevard, Suite 201

St. Anthony, MN 55418

Web site: http:www.screentalk.biz

This Web site includes interviews, how-to articles, reviews, and columns.

Screenwriter

89 5th Avenue, #123

Brooklyn, NY 11217

(718) 398-7197

Web site: http://www.screenwriter.com

The electronic version of *Screenwriter* features interviews with prominent screenwriters, agents, and producers. This site also includes reviews of movies, and software and industry news.

7

PLAYWRIGHT

The history of playwriting is a long and colorful one. The ancient Greeks considered playwriting one of the highest forms of art. They wrote plays to teach morals and values and to entertain their audiences. Today, theater productions are vastly popular all over the world, and the theater industry requires a constant influx of scripts written by playwrights from many backgrounds.

Description

Playwrights write the scripts performed by theater companies. They are sometimes directors or consultants for productions they have written. Playwrights create dramas, comedies, tragedies, mysteries, and musicals. Some break in to the business by selling their work to small-town theaters. Major cities have large theater companies.

Overall length categorizes most plays. A one-act play usually lasts no longer than thirty minutes and usually has a single setting. Theaters often show two or more one-act plays in a single evening. Full-length plays run for about an hour or two and include several scene changes. Another type of play that has become popular in recent years (mainly because of playwriting contests) is the ten-minute play. These are plays whose stories unfold and resolve quickly.

Musicals are plays accompanied by music and dancing. The actors may speak some of their lines and sing the others. Some musicals are almost completely performed in song. A team of writers and composers, rather than a single playwright, writes most musicals.

Once you have written a play, you need to find a publisher to print it or a theater company to produce it. Some

Twenty-two-year-old playwright Lauren Gunderson poses on one of the sets at the Academy Theatre in Atlanta, Georgia. A play she recently wrote, *Background*, concerns the life of Ralph Alpher, whose work in the 1940s provided the mathematics for the Big Bang theory of the beginning of the universe.

playwrights prefer to hire agents for this task. As with novels and screenplays, selling plays is a time-consuming process. You can count on rejections; this is part of the process. Most publishers and theater companies receive far more scripts than they could possibly produce. It is important for you to research the market to find the best possible publisher for your play. For instance, don't send a one-act play to publishing houses that produce only full-length plays. Most

publishers require that playwrights send a query letter before submitting a play. A few companies accept unsolicited plays. Either way, scripts must be written according to strict guidelines. Refer to the section at the end of this chapter for more information on submission guidelines.

After accepting a play, a publisher sends the playwright a contract. Once the playwright signs the contract, the publisher publishes an acting copy of the script and advertises it in its catalogue, in industry magazines, and online. Directors, producers, and theater owners browse through these scripts and select the ones they want to showcase.

Education and Training

The best training for a career as a playwright is to read and watch plays and musicals. You may benefit from entering playwriting seminars, theater workshops, and writing contests. It would also help to get a job with a theater company. Many theater companies accept volunteer interns for a variety of jobs, from building sets to securing props. Once you are working at a theater company, pay attention behind the scenes and during rehearsals.

Salary

Some playwrights receive a set payment for their plays. Many playwrights also receive royalties every time a theater performs their play, usually 25 to 50 percent of what the

Play Scripts Vs. Screenplays

Play scripts are much like screenplays in form and content, but they are also very different in some ways. Playwrights are often considered more literary or artistic in comparison to screenwriters. Screenplays are often action based, while plays are word based. That is, it is the actual writing that engages the audience. Also, less is usually more when it comes to theatrical productions. Some of the most successful plays of all time, such as *Death of a Salesman,* take place in one setting. In cases such as these, much of the drama comes from the writing and the performance. However, drama can also come from the techniques of makeup artists, fashion designers, set and lighting designers, and special-effects people. Keep this in mind when writing a play.

Plays are often much less formulaic than screenplays. As discussed in the previous chapter, most film and television producers are looking for film ideas that follow a pattern or a plot that has already been proven to work. That is why sequels are done so frequently. Playwrights, on the other hand, can usually be more inventive with their writing. Theater companies are more interested in a good story than a proven formula. Take, for example, Samuel Beckett's *Waiting for Godot,* a play about two men waiting for a third man, who in fact never shows up. Very little happens in this play, yet it is one of the most famous of all time.

Playwrights usually have much more control over their creations than do screenwriters. Playwrights sometimes make revisions to their scripts even as the play is being rehearsed on stage with actors.

publisher charges. Let's say a theater is charged $50 to show your play once, and you are entitled to 50 percent of the fee. You would get $25, and the publisher would get $25. If the theater shows the play ten times, your royalty check will be $250. Now let's say that ten theaters want to show your play ten times each. Each theater will pay you $250, for a total of $2,500. You also receive a small percentage of the money made for each acting script the publisher sells, often about 10 percent. If it sells fifty scripts at $6 a script, you receive an additional $300. The more plays you have on the market, the more royalty checks you will receive. The more recognized your name becomes, the longer your plays will run, and the more money you will earn.

Playwrights in Minneapolis, Minnesota, drink champagne out of test tubes to open the PlayLabs Festival, an annual event that features the work of unknown writers. Polly Carl *(center, wearing glasses)* is the center's artistic director.

Outlook

Playwriting is a competitive profession. Producers have literally thousands of new scripts to choose from, in addition to the classics, which never go out of style. The good news is that the theater industry is a vastly popular business that is always in need of fresh scripts. Playwrights need to be patient and persistent while they develop their craft. One of the most important things to remember when writing your script is to keep it simple. You may improve your chances of having your play produced if it contains minimal set changes and technical requirements. A play with a smaller scope may be more enticing to producers because it will cost less to produce.

FOR MORE INFORMATION

ORGANIZATIONS

The Playwrights Foundation
131 10th Street, 3rd Floor
San Francisco, CA 94103
(415) 626-0453
Web site: http://www.playwrightsfoundation.org

The Playwright's Guild of Canada
54 Wolseley Street, 2nd Floor
Toronto, ON M5T 1A5
Canada
(416) 703-0201
Web site: http://www.playwrightsguild.com

San Francisco Young Playwrights Foundation
P.O. Box 210336
San Francisco, CA 94121
(415) 794-1080
Web site: http://www.sfyoungplaywrights.org

Young Playwrights Theater (YPT)
2437 15 Street NW

Washington, DC 20009
(202) 387-9173
Web site: http://www.youngplaywrightstheater.org

Young Playwrights, Inc. (YPI)
306 W. 38th Street, Suite 300
New York, NY 10036
(212) 594-5440
Web site: http://www.youngplaywrights.org

WEB SITES
The Internet Theater Bookshop
http://www.stageplays.com
> This site provides "the most comprehensive catalog of plays in the world." This is an excellent place to browse scripts for reading or studying.

Playwrights on the Web
http://www.stageplays.com/writers.htm
> Playwrights can advertise their plays on this site, where producers and directors often come to view new work. This site also features a forum for playwrights and an e-zine.

BOOKS

Catron, Louis E. *Playwriting: Writing, Producing, and Selling Your Play.* Long Grove, IL: Waveland Press, 1990.

Cole, Toby. *Playwrights on Playwriting.* New York, NY: Cooper Square Press, 2001.

Hatcher, Jeffrey. *The Art and Craft of Playwriting.* Cincinnati, OH: Story Press Books, 2000.

McLaughlin, Buzz. *The Playwright's Process: Learning the Craft from Today's Leading Dramatists.* New York, NY: Back Stage Books, 1997.

Spencer, Stuart. *The Playwright's Guidebook: An Insightful Primer on the Art of Dramatic Writing.* London, England: Faber & Faber, 2002.

8

CHILDREN'S LITERATURE WRITER

If you've been in a bookstore lately, perhaps you have noticed that the children's section is extremely large. Magazine racks also often feature a wide range of periodicals for children of all ages. Children's literature has been popular for hundreds of years. In fact, many people believe the ancient writer Aesop wrote his fables in the sixth century BC.

Harry Potter author J. K. Rowling attends a reading of her book *Harry Potter and the Order of the Phoenix* at the Royal Albert Hall in London, England, where she greeted youngsters and signed copies of her books. Popular authors must be prepared to promote their work at public appearances, on television and radio broadcasts, and on the Internet.

It seems that children's literature is here to stay, and many people have made a good living by writing for children.

Description

The children's literature genre covers numerous types and styles of writing. Before setting out to establish a career as a children's author, you need to decide what you can offer to the children's market. Once you decide what you want to write, it will be easier to zero in on specific opportunities.

Children's magazines are extremely popular with kids. There are hundreds of freelance markets for children's magazine writers. Depending on the publication, these publishers are constantly looking for nonfiction articles, reviews, interviews, poems, and stories. Some children's magazines—such as *Highlights*—have readerships in the millions.

Children's books are equally well received. Despite the popularity of television, music, and the Internet, children's print literature continues to be a widely successful business. Children are still reading classics like *Charlie and the Chocolate Factory* and *Charlotte's Web*. New children's "classics," such as the Harry Potter series, are extremely popular. The lasting appeal of children's literature is a benefit for those hoping to establish careers as writers.

In addition to children's fiction, there is a huge nonfiction market out there for children's writers. Schools and libraries are always searching for new books on a multitude of topics: science, social studies, biographies, the arts, sports, and more. Many book publishers specialize in library books for kids.

Despite this demand, the children's book and magazine market can be competitive. Editors simply don't have enough time to read all of the manuscripts that they receive. However, as with all writers who submit their work to editors, you can get published if you have solid ideas, can express them well, and know and follow the industry standards. Writing the book or story is just half the battle. You also need to be mindful of the proper manuscript format,

Roald Dahl

Roald Dahl (1916–1990) will go down in history as one of the greatest children's writers of all time. His books are as popular today as they were when they were first released. While Dahl wrote many books for adults, it is his unique and quirky children's stories for which he is best remembered.

Dahl had a difficult early life. Both of his parents died when he was very young. Dahl's stepmother raised him and his siblings in England. When he graduated high school, Dahl did not go to college. He first worked for an oil company and sailed on ships to Africa. When World War II began, he joined the Royal Air Force (RAF) and learned how to fly fighter planes. His very first flight ended in a crash in Libya. He survived to continue fighting for the English, but he left the RAF soon after because of medical reasons.

Dahl was sent to America in 1941 to help convince America to help England win the war. His first story, "Shot Down over Libya," was published in the *Saturday Evening Post* in August 1942. This was the beginning of a long, celebrated career for Dahl.

Dahl knew how to entertain children. His stories are often creepy and grotesque, but they are always humorous. They tell the stories of lonely children, and they were written to make children laugh. Some of his greatest books include *Charlie and the Chocolate Factory*, *James and the Giant Peach*, *The BFG*, and *Matilda*. Dahl's long career is proof that children's writers can prosper without going to college, especially if they know how to think like children do.

query style, and submission guidelines. These are the skills that will allow you to get your well-crafted story into the hands of an editor who will help you shape it for publication.

Education and Training

As with all writing careers, a firm command of the English language is a must for children's authors. Everything that you send to an editor—particularly your manuscript and query letter—should be free of errors and follow standard formatting guidelines.

Reading is important for all writers, including children's authors. It is important to understand the children's writers' market and know exactly for whom you are writing. Aspiring children's authors should also read the latest

American Library Association (ALA) selection chair Eliza Dresang *(left)* holds a copy of the Newbery Medal—winning children's book *The Tale of Despereaux* as her cochair, Kathy East, holds *The Man Who Walked Between the Towers*, winner of the Caldecott Medal for Children's Illustration. Both women were in attendance at the midwinter meeting of the American Library Association in 2004.

children's books. This will help them develop their own unique style while keeping an eye on the market for what is popular and what is not.

Salary

Payment for children's books varies greatly depending on the publisher and size of the book. You could make $100 or $50,000 for your first book, depending on the publisher, the length of the book, and the age range for which you are writing.

Depending on their popularity, children's magazines may pay as little as $25 for an article or story, or as much as $1,000. They usually pay less for poetry. Some children's magazines provide only copies of the publication as payment.

Outlook

Writing for children can be challenging. While starting out may be difficult, writing for magazines can help you to break in to the book publishing business. It can also help support you as you search for the right publisher for your book. Writing nonfiction can be just as pleasing and profitable as writing fiction. As with all writers who submit work to publishers, you should be prepared for a certain amount of rejection. This is especially true of first-time authors.

FOR MORE INFORMATION

ORGANIZATIONS

Society of Children's Book Writers & Illustrators (SCBWI)
8271 Beverly Boulevard
Los Angeles, CA 90048
(323) 782-1010
Web site: http://www.scbwi.org/about.htm

The Writers' Union of Canada
90 Richmond Street East, Suite 200
Toronto, ON M5C 1P1

Canada
(416) 703-8982
Web site: http://www.writersunion.ca

WEB SITES

Children's Literature Web Guide
http://www.ucalgary.ca/~dkbrown
> A Web site devoted to Internet resources related to books for children and young adults.

Kid's Magazine Writers
http://www.kidmagwriters.com
> A great insiders' Web site that offers valuable tips from editors of children's books and magazines.

Write4Kids.com
http://www.write4kids.com
> This Web sire contains tons of articles and tips about writing for children. It also has a message board.

BOOKS

Dils, Tracey E. *You Can Write Children's Books*. Cincinnati, OH: Writer's Digest Books, 2003.

Lamb, Nancy. *The Writer's Guide for Crafting Stories for Children*. Cincinnati, OH: Writer's Digest Books, 2001.

Litowinsky, Olga. *It's a Bunny-Eat-Bunny World: A Writer's Guide to Surviving and Thriving in Today's Competitive Children's Book Market*. New York, NY: Walker & Company, 2001.

Mogilner, Alijandra. *Children's Writer's Word Book*. Cincinnati, OH: Writer's Digest Books, 1999.

Pope, Alice, ed. *2005 Children's Writer's and Illustrator's Market*. Cincinnati, OH: Writer's Digest Books, 2004.

Shepard, Aaron. *The Business of Writing for Children*. Olympia, WA: Shepard Publications, 2000.

Wyndham, Lee. *Writing for Children and Teenagers*. Cincinnati, OH: Writer's Digest Books, 2003.

PERIODICALS

Children's Book Insider
901 Columbia Road
Fort Collins, CO 80525-1838
(970) 495-0056
Web site: http://www.write4kids.com/aboutcbi.html
> A general newsletter for writers of children's books by the author of *Best Books For Kids Who (Think They) Hate to Read*.

Horn Book Magazine
56 Roland Street, Suite 200
Boston, MA 02129
(617) 628-0225
Web site: http://www.hbook.com
> A magazine that has been reporting on quality children's books and their authors since 1924.

School Library Journal
360 Park Avenue South
New York, NY 10010
(646) 746-6827
Web site: http://www.schoollibraryjournal.com
> A trade publication of the children's library book market that is commonly read by editors and publishers in the industry.

9

COPYWRITER

Our world is filled with advertisements on television, on the radio, in print, and on the Internet. Just think of how many advertisements you encounter on a daily basis: travel brochures, billboards, flyers, catalogs, radio and television commercials, infomercials, and even coupons and ads in newspapers. The abundance of advertisements shows

how important copywriters are to companies and businesses. Effective copywriters are needed to sell everything from candy bars to luxury cars.

Description

Copywriters write the words that are used in advertising. They write ad copy (the words that make up written or spoken advertisements) for all forms of media. Some copywriters write for public relations firms, marketing campaigns, or trade magazines. Freelance copywriters must be versatile enough to write copy for a wide range of products and purposes. Experienced copywriters often work for advertising agencies. In fact, the majority of advertisement work today is handled by advertising agencies.

While good writing skills are essential for copywriters, they must also be able to study a product and highlight its strongest selling points. In order to create effective copy, copywriters must research the product, the company selling it, and the people who will buy it. Much of this information often comes directly from the company for whom the copywriter works, but it never hurts to back up this information with independent research.

In general, a good copywriter must be observant, persuasive, and thoughtful. Copywriters must be able to work quickly and efficiently and are often under pressure to finish an assignment. Once a copywriter receives an assignment,

Staff writers and art directors who work at advertising agencies often start the day with a group meeting to brainstorm new ideas. Sometimes the best solutions and ad campaigns result from a group's collective effort.

he or she often has very little time to write engaging material. Many copywriters receive multiple assignments. Not only does this make deadlines more challenging, it also forces a copywriter to quickly switch from one assignment to another. A copywriter may be required to write about disposable razors one minute and frozen vegetables the next.

Deadlines are crucial. Companies expect timely results when they hire a person or a business to write copy. Newspapers are printed every day. Magazines usually come

out once a month. Television and radio ads run constantly. This continuous flow of information is created nonstop by thousands of talented writers.

Copywriters are creative writers. When it comes down to it, however, copywriters must be experts in persuasive writing. It is their job to convince people that they want the product that is being marketed. Copywriters know what people want from a product. They use this knowledge to focus their writing. Copywriters are adept at grabbing the attention of readers, viewers, and listeners with a variety of techniques. They write memorable slogans and catchy headlines. They know when to appeal to their audience's practical side and when to appeal to their emotional side.

Education and Training

While many businesses and advertising firms expect copywriters to have college degrees, this is not always the case. Many businesses will hire assistant copywriters who do not have degrees. This provides an excellent opportunity for you to get your foot in the door and start learning the ropes from experienced copywriters.

Most employers, however, will expect you to have some writing experience. Advertising agencies usually hire individuals with three to five years copy-writing experience, so you may have to work your way up to this position.

What Is an Advertising Agency?

An advertising agency is a marketing organization hired by companies to plan and create advertisements to sell their products. They are independent companies that bring a fresh perspective to their clients' products and services. An advertising agency can be very small—as few as one or two people—or it can employ hundreds of workers in many divisions. Some specialize in a particular kind of advertising, such as television commercials or Internet marketing.

Advertising agencies employ copywriters to write the text that will be used in their clients' advertisements. They may write the copy used for television commercials, radio spots, print advertisements, packaging, billboards, brochures, and so on. Sometimes they are assigned multiple projects at the same time. Copywriters working for agencies may also be required to create a central theme that will be used in a series of commercials and print advertising for the same product or company. Creating a central theme in an advertising campaign means that a client's product or service will be easily recognized by consumers across a variety of markets for extended periods.

Whether working for an ad agency, publishing house, newspaper, or magazine, writers must always consider the photographs and illustrations that appear beside their text. In this image, students weigh the validity and impact of potential images for an advertising campaign.

Copywriters who create copy for print media may also want to familiarize themselves with standard graphic arts techniques and computer programs. This will help them to better visualize the finished product as they write. It will also make it easier for them to work hand-in-hand with the graphic artists who will be transforming their words into visual advertisements.

Salary

Assistant copywriters may start at about $25,000 to $27,000 a year or more. Once you work your way up to copywriter, however, you can make between $30,000 and $80,000, or perhaps more, depending on the company and your experience. The most successful copywriters can make a six-figure income, but this takes years of experience.

Outlook

Copywriting and advertising jobs are plentiful in our consumer-oriented society. However, this does not mean that becoming a copywriter is an easy task. The job market can be fierce, and copywriters need both experience and confidence to succeed. Plan to start out on the low end of the pay scale. Many copywriters begin this way, and many succeed. Be observant, persistent, and confident in your abilities.

FOR MORE INFORMATION

ORGANIZATIONS

American Marketing Association
311 South Wacker Drive, Suite 5800
Chicago, IL 60606
(800) 262-1150
Web site: http://www.marketingpower.com

WEB SITES

AdCopyWriting.com

http://www.adcopywriting.com

This site features valuable advice from a successful copywriter and advertising veteran. It includes educational information on various aspects of copywriting and marketing, plus a newsletter called the *Copywriter's Digest*.

Excess Voice

http://www.excessvoice.com/index.htm

This Web site features articles in a newsletter format on various topics of interest to copywriters and those interested in pursuing a career in the field.

Writing Smart

http://www.writing-smart.com/copywriter.html

This concise yet thorough Web site contains helpful tips and resources about working in advertising.

BOOKS

Bly, Robert. *The Copywriter's Handbook: A Step-by-Step Guide to Writing Copy That Sells*. New York, NY: Henry Holt and Company, 1990.

Gabay, J. Jonathan. *Teach Yourself Copywriting*. New York, NY: McGraw-Hill, 2003.

Ogilvy, David. *Ogilvy on Advertising*. New York, NY: Vintage, 1985.

Pricken, Mario. *Creative Advertising: Ideas and Techniques from the World's Best Campaigns*. New York, NY: Thames & Hudson, 2004.

Sant, Tom. *Persuasive Business Proposals: Writing to Win More Customers, Clients, and Contracts*. New York, NY: AMACOM, 2003.

Schwab, Victor O. *How to Write a Good Advertisement.* Chatsworth, CA: Wilshire Book Company, 1985.

PUBLIC RELATIONS ASSISTANT

You may have heard the expression "Looks aren't everything," but in the worlds of business and politics, looks *are* everything. If a company does something that looks bad in the eyes of the public, people may boycott the company. If a politician says or does the wrong thing, he or she may lose votes or popularity. Needless to say, this is the opposite of what a company or politician wants. In these cases, powerful public relations can work wonders to save a company from going under or to get a politician elected to office.

Description

Public relations assistants communicate directly with the public or the media for the purpose of expressing company opinions, policies, or responses to public concerns. They also receive and respond to complaints made by members of the public or by public service organizations. It is a public relations assistant's job to present the company for whom he or she works in a favorable light. Public relations assistants are also sometimes needed to repair reputations that have been damaged in the eyes of the public.

Anyone or any group that is interested in portraying a positive image to the general public may hire a public relations assistant. They work for public figures and celebrities, politicians, government agencies, companies, advertising agencies, associations, nonprofit organizations, colleges, television stations, and hospitals. Some public relations assistants work for consulting firms and are assigned to cover individual events for clients. Others might be specialists in a specific area, such as children's groups or sports figures.

Public relations assistants usually report to public relations managers or executives. The executives are those workers who are in direct contact with company management. The

Model Naomi Campbell holds a lunch box she designed as she arrives for a charity auction that will offer lunch boxes designed by celebrities to benefit the Lunch Box Fund and the Food Bank of New York City. Public relations executives often work directly with celebrities for charity functions or other campaigns that require a lot of public exposure.

executives relay information to the assistants and inform them how to proceed. In many cases, the executives receive the credit for the work that public relations assistants accomplish. For instance, executives may give speeches written by assistants, or they may use copy written by assistants in press conferences.

Public relations assistants need solid writing skills. In many ways, the public relations assistant is much like the copywriter. Both must sell their company and its goods and/or services. Public relations specialists write text for speeches, press releases, newsletters, advertisements, shareholder reports, employee handbooks, magazine articles, and more.

In addition to these duties, public relations assistants may be required to schedule fund-raisers, give speeches and interviews, organize meetings and conventions, investigate complaints, mediate discussions, and create promotional and training videos. Public relations workers must be excellent leaders with solid communications skills. They must also be familiar with modern business practices.

Education and Training

Many employers prefer public relations assistants with college degrees, but that isn't always necessary. Experience in journalism, copywriting, or advertising may often lead to a position as a public relations assistant.

You can prepare for a public relations job in high school by working for your school newspaper and/or television station. Volunteering to work on political campaigns may also help. While you are still in high school, having a retail job can help you form solid selling techniques. Many public relations assistants begin their careers as news reporters or as interns or secretaries for public relations firms.

It is often jokingly said that people who work in public relations are only as valuable as their contacts, because a PR assistant's contacts are often the key to his or her success. In order to be successful in this industry, you need to have an upbeat personality. Most people in public relations love working with others, getting people together, networking and gathering resources, and talking on the phone to clients and representatives.

Public relations workers who have been working in the field for five years can take a certification course that is administered by the Public Relations Society of America. By doing this, a person can use the term "accredited in public relations" when describing his or her experience.

Salary

An entry-level public relations assistant may start as low as $15,000 a year, depending on his or her experience. However, this number usually increases quickly, especially after he or she has proven to be a competent writer. The salary range for public relations workers is broad. While the average salary is between $45,000 and $55,000, it could be as high as $150,000.

Outlook

Individuals looking for work in the public relations field are often assigned low-responsibility duties, such as taking polls or collecting research. Moving up the ladder may take some time because the skills you need take time to master. The more experience you have, the more responsibility you will receive. Some public relations assistants wait for promotions in the company for which they work, while others prefer to change companies when they have gained sufficient experience. If you gain enough knowledge and expertise in a specific field, you may decide to become an independent consultant. This option, however, takes a great deal of experience. The good news is that there are thousands of companies that require public relations workers of every level.

FOR MORE INFORMATION

ORGANIZATIONS

Institute for Public Relations (IPR)
P.O. Box 118400
2096 Weimer Hall
Gainesville, FL 32611-8400
(352) 92-0280
Web site: http://www.instituteforpr.com

Public Relations Society of America
33 Maiden Lane, 11th Floor
New York, NY 10038-5150
(212) 460-1400
Web site: http://www.prsa.org

WEB SITES

All About Public Relations
http://aboutpublicrelations.net
> This Web site contains an archive of articles about public relations topics, a comprehensive resource list, and a general reference library. It also contains information about career development.

Online Public Relations
http://www.online-pr.com
> This site contains a wealth of information about careers in the public relations industry, including links for research and reference as well as tons of resources.

BOOKS

Aronson, Merry, and Don Spetner. *The Public Relations Writer's Handbook*. New York, NY: Jossey-Bass, 1998.

Blake, Gary, and Robert W. Bly. *The Elements of Business Writing: A Guide to Writing Clear, Concise Letters, Memos, Reports, Proposals, and Other Business Documents.* Boston, MA: Pearson Education, 1992.

Levine, Michael. *Guerrilla P.R. Wired: Waging a Successful Publicity Campaign Online, Offline, and Everywhere In Between.* New York, NY: McGraw-Hill, 2002.

McIntyre, Catherine V. *Writing Effective News Releases . . . :How to Get Free Publicity for Yourself, Your Business, or Your Organization.* Colorado Springs, CO: Piccadilly Books, 1992.

Wilcox, Dennis L. *Public Relations Writing and Media Techniques.* Boston, MA: Allyn & Bacon, 2004.

Yale, David R., and Andrew J. Carothers. *The Publicity Handbook.* New York, NY: McGraw-Hill, 2001.

PERIODICALS

PR Week
Haymarket Media
114 W. 26th Street, 3rd Floor
New York, NY 10001
(646) 638-6000
Web site: http://www.prweek.com
This is the Web site of the weekly trade publication of the public relations industry. This site features articles, interviews, and a jobs board.

Strategist
33 Maiden Lane, 11th Floor
New York, NY 10038-5150
Web site: http://www.prsa.org
This is the Web site of the trade magazine of the Public Relations Society of America. It contains information on professional career development, industry conferences and seminars, jobs, and general news.

COPY EDITOR

Would you buy a television from a store after reading a sign in its window that said, "No won can beet our prices"? Perhaps you would—especially if the prices really were unbeatable—but chances are you would think twice about buying anything from a store that couldn't spell the words on its own sign. Writing copy is a job for

copywriters. Correcting and perfecting that copy is a job for copy editors.

This career is best for people who are knowledgeable, determined, and passionate about everything they do. This is a job for individuals who make informed, sensible decisions, and then stand by those decisions. That is not to say that copy editors won't admit when they are wrong, but they are seldom wrong, and they know it.

Description

Copy editors work for book publishers, magazines, and newspapers. Also, nearly every company that creates advertisements uses the services of copy editors. They make sure that the writing for soon-to-be-published pieces is as accurate as possible. Copy editors examine spelling, grammar, style, and the slant of the writing. Copy editors work quickly and efficiently, and they must have good communication skills.

Copy editors have a strong understanding of the industry in which they work, as well as the style guide and practices of the company for which they work. A newspaper copy editor should know how to write headlines and captions. Copy editors who work for book publishers should know how to create an index. In other words, they need to become familiar with the entire publishing process. Many copy editors are expected to understand typesetting codes, which they often

Talented copy editors are intelligent and versatile. They need to have a good attitude, work well with others, and understand the necessity of meeting deadlines. Most copy editors are also required to keep up with current events and trends.

write directly in the margins of the piece of writing they are copyediting.

Equally important is a sense of curiosity. Copy editors always want to know more, and they spend a good deal of time researching and exploring a wide range of topics—even in their spare time. This constant pursuit of knowledge is what makes copy editors good at what they do. Vital to a copy editor's job is a wide range of reference materials: dictionaries, encyclopedias, atlases, style books, and many others.

Many employers like to hire copy editors who can offer creative suggestions on how to correct errors. This could mean changing a few words or rewriting an entire paragraph. Creative thinking can help copy editors save time and meet deadlines. Copy editors often make suggestions for the design team as well.

Copyediting is often thought of as a thankless job. Copy editors are responsible for pointing out changes that need to be made late in the production schedule, after editors and writers have crafted what they think is a flawless piece of writing. Nevertheless, copy editors are detail-oriented professionals who know the obscure rules of grammar and language. They notice the minor errors that others are too busy to see.

When applying for a job as a copy editor, it is important to know something about the company offering the job and its publication. If you are applying for a job at a newspaper, for example, be sure to read as many copies of that paper as possible. Become familiar with the layout, the columns, and the writers. The same goes for magazine and book publishers. Familiarize yourself with the company and its product.

Education and Training

Most employers expect you to have some experience before hiring you as a copy editor. This is not always the case, as long as you have strong language skills, enthusiasm for the

Copyediting Symbols

The following list shows a sample of common symbols and abbreviations used by copy editors to convey information to editors, writers, and designers. These symbols are written directly on printed proofs, usually in the margins, and are meant as directions for revision.

Symbol	Meaning	Symbol	Meaning
∨ ∧	insert text or punctuation	ℂ	paragraph
℘	delete	℘	delete and close space
ⓒap	capitalize	⌒⌣	close up space
ⓛc	lowercase	# ∧	insert space
⩳ ∧	insert hyphen	ⓢtet	Leave text as is
ⓢp	check spelling	ⓣr	transpose (reverse) letters/words

job, and a willingness to learn. Employers who are looking for copy editors often want people who are thorough, confident, and knowledgeable about everyday events.

Some companies will expect you to have experience with graphic arts computer programs. Not all, however, will expect this type of experience, and many will even teach you specific software programs on the job.

Salary

Although beginning copy editors often start at about $25,000, inexperienced copy editors may have to settle for a smaller salary. Larger companies may start a copy editor at about $30,000. Freelancers may make more, depending on how much work they do. You may eventually earn $60,000 or more, depending on the publication for which you work and your experience.

Outlook

Nearly every book publisher, magazine, and newspaper has at least one copy editor, though many have an entire department or team of copy editors. Competition for these jobs can be fierce. An adept copy editor can work his or her way up to managing editor or editor in chief if he or she sets his or her mind to it.

FOR MORE INFORMATION

ORGANIZATIONS

American Copy Editors Society (ACES)
11690B Sunrise Valley Drive
Reston, VA 20191-1409
(703) 453-1122
Web site: http://www.copydesk.org

Modern Language Association (MLA)
26 Broadway, 3rd Floor
New York, NY 10004-1789
(646) 576-5000
Web site: http://www.mla.org

WEB SITES

Grammar Now!
http://www.grammarnow.com
  A quick guide to grammar, usage, and editing.

Guide to Grammar and Style
http://andromeda.rutgers.edu/~jlynch/Writing/index.html
  The Web site style guide by an associate professor of English at Rutgers University in New Jersey includes a guide to grammar rules.

Owl: Online Writing Lab—Editing and Proofreading Strategies
http://owl.english.purdue.edu/handouts/general/gl_edit.html
  This comprehensive Web site by the Purdue University Online Writing Lab contains valuable information on editing and revising any type of written work.

The Slot: A Spot for Copy Editors
http://www.theslot.com

The Slot includes a blog by Bill Walsh, author of *The Elephant Style* and copy editor of the *Washington Post*.

Testy Copy Editors
http://www.testycopyeditors.org
> A general discussion board where copy editors talk shop and debate various points.

BOOKS

Camp, Sue C. *Developing Proofreading and Editing Skills*. New York, NY: Irwin/McGraw-Hill, 2000.

Judd, Karen. *Copyediting: A Practical Guide.* Menlo Park, CA: Crisp Publications, 2001.

Larocque, Paul. *The Concise Guide to Copy Editing: Preparing Written Work for Readers*. Oak Park, IL: Marion Street Press, 2003.

Rooney, Edmund J., and Oliver R. Witte. *Copy Editing for Professionals.* Champaign, IL: Stipes Publishing, 2000.

Stainton, Elsie Myer. *The Fine Art of Copyediting*. New York, NY: Columbia University Press, 2002.

PERIODICALS

Copy Editor
McMurry Campus Center
1010 East Missouri Avenue
Phoenix, AZ 85014
http://www.copyeditor.com/copy/copy.asp
> The industry magazine contains information about working in the publishing industry and helps copy editors keep up-to-date about changes in their field.

FACT-CHECKER

Do you have a photographic memory? Do you remember seemingly irrelevant facts and figures? Besides becoming a regular contestant on the game show *Jeopardy!* you many want to think about a career as a fact- checker. A fact-checker is a valuable addition to any editorial staff. Fact-checkers are often the first line of defense when it comes to identifying incorrect statistics, name spellings, dates, information surrounding historical events, and up-to-date contact information. Fact-checkers often assist editors and copy editors so that they can accomplish their jobs with greater speed and accuracy.

Description

The Pulitzer Prize–winning writer and columnist Ellen Goodman once wrote, "In journalism, there has always been a tension between getting it first and getting it right." Goodman is pointing out that the words that we read in the newspaper are not always truthful. Some news reporters and journalists get so caught up in the race to be first that they forget (or simply neglect) to be right. Writers, editors, copy editors, and proofreaders all help to create factual news stories and articles. Fact-checkers base their entire careers on getting accurate information.

Fact-checkers have a lot of responsibility. It is their duty to help the publication for which they work to avoid litigation resulting from printing incorrect or biased information. At the same time, fact-checkers often need to work swiftly, leaving little time to double-check articles or manuscripts for accuracy. Most publications take pride in providing information. Retractions are a great source of embarrassment for any newspaper, magazine, or publishing house.

This librarian from Paramus, New Jersey, helps a college student locate facts in a reference book. Doing research in a library and seeking assistance from qualified reference librarians are sometimes part of a fact-checker's job.

Fact-checkers constantly learn new information and build upon previous knowledge. They learn as they work and even get a thrill from solving problems. Books of all kinds are very important to the fact-checker's job, from dictionaries and encyclopedias to more specialized resources, such as medical books and art history texts. Other forms of information that fact-checkers use on a daily basis include online resources, telephone contacts, and alliances with writers and editors. Fact-checkers quickly build a large collection of resources that they can consult at a moment's notice.

Fact-checkers need to keep an open mind. Although fact-checkers might be very experienced and knowledgeable in many areas, there are always instances when they must investigate a field with which they are unfamiliar. Fact-checkers must work with writers, editors, copy editors, designers, and others when preparing text for publication. It only makes the process more difficult when one of those workers refuses to accept input from the others. Regardless of how good a fact-checker is, he or she should always be open to suggestions from other members of the editorial staff. A good fact-checker also knows when to seek the help of others.

Despite the work of a large team of editors, proofreaders, and fact-checkers, mistakes still manage to slip through the cracks. Criticism for these errors often falls on the fact-checkers. Don't get upset about criticism. Instead, investigate the errors and learn the truth.

Education and Training

It's obvious that a solid understanding of the English language will help you succeed as a fact-checker. It also helps to read as much as you can. Knowledge—any kind of knowledge—will help you to save time since you will spend less time searching for information.

A good way to train for a career as a fact-checker is to scan the daily newspaper for errors every day. Researching facts and finding mistakes will give you a taste of what it is like to be a professional fact-checker.

Salary

Beginning fact-checkers may make about $25,000 to $30,000 a year. They make more with experience, and even more if they are promoted to higher positions. Freelancers usually make between $20 and $30 an hour. They sometimes make more, depending on the content of the publication.

Outlook

Becoming a fact-checker is often a starting point in a person's editorial career. You may move from fact-checker to copy editor, editor, or reporter, and then on to a position as managing or senior editor. Others have long careers as fact-checkers.

In general, any company that prints nonfiction might benefit from an on-staff fact-checker. Depending on the size of the publication, fact-checking may be the responsibility of editors, copy editors, and/or proofreaders. Daily newspapers do not hire fact-checkers because there simply is no time for them to do their job. Newspapers often expect their reporters and editors to check facts. Weekly news magazines like *Time* are more likely to hire fact-checkers.

Many fact-checkers make excellent money as freelancers. Some specialize in a certain areas of publishing, such as educational books and materials. Some will tackle a variety of material, especially if the price is right. Many

publishers prefer to use freelance fact-checkers because it is cheaper to hire them as they are needed rather than pay full-time employees.

Fact-checkers need a wide range of resources to do their jobs well. Years ago, fact-checkers spent long hours between dusty library stacks. Today—thanks to modern innovations like the Internet—fact-checkers have reference materials at their fingertips at all times.

Working as a fact-checker sometimes means double- and triple-checking material that is referenced in an article or manuscript. In some cases, fact-checkers reach out to other professionals for opinions about information that directly relates to their business or field.

FOR MORE INFORMATION

WEB SITES

American Press Institute (API)
http://www.americanpressinstitute.org/content/3899.cfm
> This Web site offers an extensive list of Internet sources where accurate information is available to professional fact-checkers and anyone who wants to check printed information.

Fact Checkers and Copy Editors
http://parklibrary.jomc.unc.edu/factcheckers2004.html
> This Web site contains plenty of resources and a reference "tool kit."

FactCheck.org
http://www.factcheck.org
> An excellent Web site from the Annenberg Public Policy Center of the University of Pennsylvania where writers can check political facts.

FedStats
http://www.fedstats.gov
> This Web site offers a search engine with the ability to locate information, statistics, and maps related to or previously published by any federal agency.

Freeality
http://www.freeality.com
> A listing of Internet search engines.

Google
http://www.google.com
> An excellent all-purpose Web site that anyone can use easily and quickly.

Library of Congress Wise Guide

http://www.loc.gov/wiseguide/index-flash.html

This Web portal, part of the Web site of the U.S. Library of Congress offers a search engine to locate specific items in the library's database.

Refdesk.com

http://www.refdesk.com

A comprehensive Web site with a variety of sources to check facts.

BOOKS

Amster, Linda, and Dylan Loeb McClain, eds. *Kill Duck Before Serving: Red Faces at the New York Times*. New York, NY: St. Martin's Press, 2002.

Hock, Randolph. *The Extreme Searcher's Internet Handbook: A Guide for the Serious Searcher*. Medford, NJ: CyberAge Books, 2004.

Merriam-Webster. *Merriam Webster's Manual for Writers and Editors*. Springfield, MA: Merriam-Webster, 1998.

Mintz, Anne P., ed. *Web of Deception: Misinformation on the Internet*. Medford, NJ: Information Today, 2002.

Smith, Sarah Harrison. *The Fact Checker's Bible: A Guide to Getting It Right*. New York, NY: Anchor Books, 2004.

SECRETARY

When you think of someone in a secretarial position, do you picture an older women wearing a sweater and taking notes? Don't let the stereotype fool you: secretarial work can be challenging, fulfilling, and even exciting. Among the many skills a secretary will need, writing is one of the most important. Today, secretaries are

also commonly known as administrative or executive assistants.

Description

Secretaries, or administrative assistants, assist other workers with a wide range of responsibilities. Secretaries are a vital component to our modern business world. Many businesses and corporations rely on secretaries to keep their organizations running smoothly. Without them, many offices would fall apart.

Depending on the company for which they work, secretaries may do any or all of the following tasks: answer phones, greet clients and answer their questions, write letters and reports, edit documents, book travel plans, order office supplies, train new employees, set up meetings, take notes, take dictation, use and maintain office machines, schedule appointments, organize and update records, and handle payroll and bookkeeping tasks. In general, secretaries make sure the day-to-day activities of an office run smoothly. In doing their job, secretaries allow supervisors, managers, and other employees to perform their own jobs more efficiently.

Some secretarial positions require specialized skills. For example, a secretary who works for a real estate office must know how to close a sale on a house and must understand the jargon and paperwork specific to the real estate business.

Administrative assistants answer questions, direct people around the office, take and forward telephone calls, and manage a variety of office details.

Legal secretaries must know how to take specific information from clients and are often the people who interview clients before an attorney is even called in to review a case.

Secretaries are usually under pressure to perform quickly and efficiently. Some work for several managers or supervisors, while others work for just one. Some may be expected to work long hours or to travel frequently. Whatever their situation, secretaries need to be cooperative, organized, and dependable. They need to be able to fulfill a

request quickly without asking how to get it done. Secretaries are often thought of as problem-solvers. When the photocopier breaks down, for instance, adept secretaries know how to get it working again. If they cannot fix the problem themselves, they quickly contact a person who can. This type of reaction to office problems allows supervisors and managers to continue working with as few interruptions as possible.

People skills are very important for secretaries. They must be able to communicate clearly and professionally, in person and on the telephone. Individuals who get nervous when talking to clients and supervisors may not make it very long as secretaries, regardless of how well they perform their daily tasks.

There are many kinds of writing in which a secretary must be proficient. Writing effective business letters is only one facet of the job. He or she must also write reports, invoices, memos, schedules, notes, and much more. Secretaries must have effective writing skills, must be proficient at many types of software, and must be able to write any of the aforementioned documents at a moment's notice.

Education and Training

High school instruction in math, English, and business will help prepare you for a job as a secretary. Most employers expect their secretaries to be familiar with computers and standard business software. It may also help to have a basic understanding of computer hardware. Secretaries need efficient typing skills (at least sixty words per minute) and may also need to know shorthand, for writing important information in a hurry. Having a working knowledge of these topics will surely give you a leg up on other job applicants.

Many secretaries take classes and receive certification as professional secretaries, which increases their chances of finding jobs that pay well. You can learn more about secretary certification through the organizations listed at the end of this chapter.

Salary

Salaries for secretaries depend on several factors, including the employer, the type of business, and the secretary's level of experience. Beginning secretaries with no specialized experience may earn about $18,000 to $20,000 a year. Experienced secretaries may earn a salary of about $40,000 a year. Secretaries working for important executives may make $50,000 or more. In general, any secretarial experience that you have will increase your annual salary.

Outlook

The outlook for secretarial careers is very good. In fact, theirs is among the quickest-growing occupations in

Secretarial positions are not only for women. More and more men are now taking jobs as administrative professionals. For some people, working in an office environment is a fulfilling experience that offers great benefits and a solid foundation for a variety of future positions.

America. Think of all the businesses in your town or city that depend on secretaries to keep things running smoothly. There are plenty of secretarial jobs to go around, but it is the most conscientious and skillful secretaries who meet with the greatest success. Some secretaries are promoted to managerial positions once they have been with a company long enough and understand how it works.

PROFILE

Amanda Smith has been an administrative assistant for a construction company for two years. She has also worked as an administrative assistant for a multimillion-dollar telecommunications company and as a medical office assistant.

WHAT DO YOU LIKE BEST ABOUT YOUR JOB?

I enjoy dealing with many different people, from the common homeowner to savvy businessmen and businesswomen. Also, knowing that I helped someone feel more comfortable and happier with their new surroundings, whether it is their home, office, cottage, garage, or deck, is a great feeling.

WHAT DO YOU LIKE LEAST ABOUT YOUR JOB?

Some people that I deal with are not very friendly. There are a lot of people out there who will try to get out of paying for things. I believe that you get what you pay for. If you want quality work, there is a price. That is why it is so important that a contract is drawn up to protect the contractor, the homeowner, or the business owner.

WHAT ADVICE WOULD YOU GIVE TO SOMEONE WHO WAS THINKING ABOUT PURSUING A CAREER AS AN ADMINISTRATIVE ASSISTANT?

Make sure that you are a people person, someone who likes to interact with all kinds of people. Strive to be an efficient self-motivator. Try not to loose your cool. Always

remember that you have to be held accountable for your actions, or things you might say in anger.

HOW IS WRITING IMPORTANT TO YOUR JOB?

I need to write the invoices that are received by our customers. I generate monthly reports for our accountant that must be precise and worded professionally. I create spreadsheets for the materials we buy and use on jobs. Each week, I need to document the work hours for each employee and appoint his or her time to the correct job for invoicing. I also have to document the money coming in and going out, including the payroll and monthly bills.

FOR MORE INFORMATION

ORGANIZATIONS

American Management Association
1601 Broadway
New York, NY 10019
(212) 586-8100
Web site: http://www.amanet.org/index.htm

International Association of Administrative Professionals (IAAP)
10502 NW Ambassador Drive
P.O. Box 20404
Kansas City, MO 64195-0404
(816) 891-6600
Web site: http://www.iaap-hq.org

National Association of Executive Secretaries and Administrative Assistants (NAESAA)
900 S. Washington Street, Suite G-13
Falls Church, VA 22046
(703) 237-8616
Web site: http://www.naesaa.com

Professional Secretaries International (PSI)
10502 NW Ambassador Drive
P.O. Box 20404
Kansas City, MO 64195-0404
(816) 891-6600
Web site: http://www.main.org/psi

WEB SITES

Adminassist.com
http://www.adminassist.ca
> This Web site contains information, resources, and job listings for administrative professionals in Canada.

Association of Administrative Assistants (AAA)
http://www.aaa.ca
> The Association of administrative Assistants is a chartered, non-profit Canadian organization founded in 1951.

Desk Demon
http://us.deskdemon.com/pages/us/indexus
> This useful Web site contains articles about administrative careers, resources, forums, and job opportunities.

Wikipedia: Shorthand
http://en.wikipedia.org/wiki/Shorthand
> This Web site offers a concise explanation of shorthand for office workers.

BOOKS

Jaderstrom, Susan, et al. *Complete Office Handbook*. New York, NY: Random House Reference, 2002.

Lindsell-Roberts, Sheryl. *Mastering Computer Typing: A Painless Course for Beginners and Professionals*. Boston, MA: Houghton Mifflin, 1995.

Merriam-Webster. *Merriam-Webster's Guide to Business Correspondence*. Springfield, MA: Merriam-Webster, 1996.

Merriam-Webster. *Professional Secretary's Encyclopedic Dictionary*. Upper Saddle River, NJ: Prentice Hall, 1994.

Piotrowski, Maryann V. *Effective Business Writing: A Guide for Those Who Write on the Job*. New York, NY: HarperCollins Publishers, 1996.

Stroman, James, et al. *Administrative Assistant's and Secretary's Handbook*. New York, NY: AMACOM, 2003.

PARALEGAL

The legal profession is a growing industry. Lawyers are necessary for a long list of legal matters, from criminal trials to business transactions. The duties that attorneys have are many, and our legal system would come to a grinding halt if it weren't for the hard work and dedication of paralegals.

Description

Paralegals are also known as legal assistants because they assist lawyers in delivering legal services. Paralegals are seen as a necessary, time-saving component of our legal system. Lawyers usually take on the bulk of legal work, including interviewing clients and witnesses, giving legal advice, setting fees, accepting clients, and trying cases in a court of law. These are tasks for which legal assistants are not trained, and in fact, it is against the law for them to carry out those activities.

However, these are just a few of the duties related to legal work. Paralegals complete a wide range of tasks that lawyers simply don't have time to complete on their own. In general, paralegals help lawyers prepare for court cases, hearings, estate closings, will readings, and meetings. Some of the specific duties included in their job are researching past cases, investigating a current case to ensure the legal team has the facts straight, interviewing witnesses, analyzing and organizing information, and general administrative work. Legal assistants sometimes gather data under the supervision of a lawyer. Paralegal work almost always entails a long list of writing duties, including writing reports and letters, preparing legal arguments, and drafting contracts.

The law firm of Scolaro, Shulman, Cohen, Fetter & Burstein finds it effective to hire lawyers who worked there as paralegals and students. The firm employs Ann Ealy *(left)*, a second-year law student at Stanford University, and Carol Christiansen *(right)*, a lawyer who was formerly a paralegal.

Law firms and government offices employ paralegals. Paralegals are also hired by corporations that have their own legal departments, such as Microsoft, United Airlines, and McDonalds, to name just a few. While the jobs of many paralegals often entail many or most of the duties listed in the previous paragraph, some tasks are more particular. Some legal assistants function more like secretaries, with minimal legal work involved. Others specialize in a small area of legal work, such as preparing the necessary paperwork

for real estate closings. Regardless of the focus of the job, writing skills are almost always necessary.

Paralegal jobs can be stressful. Deadlines for reports and projects are usually strict, and if the workload is large enough, legal assistants will be expected to work long hours. Some are expected to travel frequently. Fortunately, most paralegals are rewarded for their hard work with excellent benefits, including vacation time and bonus pay. Despite the high level of stress related to paralegal jobs, they can also be exciting and fulfilling. Legal assistants meet many people and encounter many stories as they do their jobs.

Education and Training

Without a college degree, you will most likely have to work your way up to a position as a paralegal. Since basic paralegal work is similar in some ways to secretarial work, gaining employment as a legal secretary or administrative assistant is excellent training. Many law firms offer on-the-job training. Those interested in becoming a paralegal can complete a paralegal certification program and receive the title of registered paralegal, although most employers will not expect this certificate. (You can find more information about certification courses from the organizations in the directory at the end of this chapter.) Still others may be hired because they have mastered a specific skill, such as filing tax returns.

Salary

Salary for a legal assistant depends on several criteria, including the size of the business or law firm, training and experience, and the geographic location of the job. Beginning legal assistants may make about $30,000. Experienced paralegals may make between $45,000 and $60,000, or more. The federal government is the largest employer of legal assistants in the United States and pays them an average of about $55,000. Local and state governments pay legal assistants an average of about $35,000.

Outlook

Paralegal positions are numerous and are expected to remain so in the future. However, as mentioned previously, these jobs may be difficult to attain without a college degree. That does not mean you should give up hope of ever becoming a paralegal. Training in other jobs can help you to move up if you take the time to learn the skills necessary to work in a law office.

Rebecca Valois, from Centreville, Virginia, has studied law for three years at the private Virginia practice of her mother-in-law, Judith Valois. The latter was admitted to the state bar in 1986 after getting her legal education from her husband. They are part of a small group of "law readers"—people who study law in offices or judges' chambers rather than in classrooms.

FOR MORE INFORMATION

ORGANIZATIONS

Legal Secretaries International, Inc.
2302 Fannin Street, Suite 500
Houston, TX 77002-9136
Web site: http://www.legalsecretaries.org

The National Association of Legal Assistants
1516 S. Boston, #200
Tulsa, OK 74119
(918) 587-6828
Web site: http://www.nala.org

National Association for Legal Secretaries (NALS)
314 East 3rd Street, Suite 210
Tulsa, OK 74120
(918) 582-5188
Web site: http://www.nals.org

The National Federation of Paralegal Associations
2517 Eastlake Avenue East, Suite 200
Seattle, WA 98102
(206) 652-4120
Web site: http://www.paralegals.org

WEB SITES

The Concise Law Encyclopedia
http://www.TheLawEncyclopedia.com
> This comprehensive site is a good place for young people to familiarize themselves with legal phrasing and issues that relate to the judicial process.

Legal Definitions

http://www.legal-definitions.com

This Web site is a great reference for learning legal terms and phrases.

BOOKS

DeVries, Mary A. *Legal Secretary's Complete Handbook*. Upper Saddle River, NJ: Prentice Hall, 1992.

Garner, Bryan A., ed. *Black's Law Dictionary*. Second Pocket Edition. Eagan, MN: West Publishing, 2004.

Garner, Bryan A. *Legal Writing in Plain English: A Text with Exercises*. Chicago, IL: University of Chicago Press, 2001.

Gifis, Steven H. *Dictionary of Legal Terms: A Simplified Guide to the Language of Law*. Hauppauge, NY: Barron's Educational Series, 1998.

Morton, Joyce. *Legal Office Procedures*. Upper Saddle River, NJ: Prentice Hall, 2003.

Smith, Nancy Creel, and Tracy Rives Johnston. *Legal Document Production*. Upper Saddle River, NJ: Prentice Hall, 1996.

Von Matt Stoddard, Sonia. *The Legal Assistant's Letter Book*. Upper Saddle River, NJ: Prentice Hall, 1995.

GLOSSARY

adaptation A work of writing that has been rewritten into a new form.

administrative Relating to the management of business matters.

agent An expert in a field, such as book publishing, who acts on behalf of a client; a business representative.

beat The specific neighborhood or area that a newspaper writer

reports on for his or her job. For a small paper, a beat could be an entire town.

deadline The time at which a project must be completed.

dictate To speak or read to a person so he or she can record the words in writing.

documentary A movie based on factual, documented evidence.

executive Having the function of managing or carrying out plans or orders.

formula In writing and publishing, this is often the set structure of a book or article.

freelance To pursue a career without working for any one company or publication.

graphic design The art or profession of using design elements (such as pictures and text) to convey meaning.

impromptu Something that is unplanned or spontaneous.

influx A mass arrival or incoming.

internship A position in the publishing industry that acts as a support to the editorial staff. Internships are normally unpaid positions.

jargon The specialized or technical language of a trade or profession.

periodical A serial publication with a fixed interval of time between issues.

press release An official document issued to reporters and writers about a specific topic, usually something newsworthy, or to launch a product, film, book, promotional campaign, etc.

proof A sheet of paper filled with text that is meant to be compared to an earlier form with the purpose of finding and marking errors.

Pulitzer prize An annual award in the United States for journalists, writers, and musical composers established by journalist and newspaper publisher Joseph Pulitzer (1847–1911).

query letter A formal letter meant to introduce a writer and his or her work to an agent, editor, or publisher.

retraction A correction for something that was printed that was incorrect.

royalties Money paid to the creator of a work of art for the use of that work of art.

scrutinize To examine closely.

seminar A meeting for an exchange of ideas; a conference.

sequel In film, a movie that continues the story of a preceding movie.

style guide A book detailing a standard way of writing.

syndicate A group of publications that share news stories and/or articles.

synopsis A concise summary of a film, book, etc.

technique A method of accomplishing a goal.

trade magazine A magazine that discusses the developments of a particular industry.

typesetting The processing of preparing written words for printing.

unbiased Free from prejudice or favoritism.

unsolicited Referring to something submitted to, but not requested by, a publisher.

INDEX

About the Author

Greg Roza has a bachelor's degree and a master's degree in English from the State University of New York at Fredonia. His entire career has since focused on authoring and editing books for both children and adults. He lives with his wife, Abigail; daughter, Autumn; and son, Lincoln, in upstate New York.

Photo Credits

Cover © Photodisc/Getty Images; pp. 9, 14, 128, 130 © David Lassman/Syracuse Newspapers/The Image Works; p. 10 © Kevin Fleming/Corbis; pp. 21, 27 © Tom Stewart/Corbis; p. 22 © AP/ Wide World Photos/Jim Cooper; pp. 31, 36 © AP/Wide World Photos/New Haven Register/Melanie Stengel; p. 32 © AP/Wide World Photos/Scott Suchman; pp. 40, 45 © AP/Wide World Photos Tony Dejak; p. 42 © Will Waldron/The Image Works; pp. 49, 50 © AP/Wide World Photos/Tim Boyd; p. 53 © AP/Wide World Photos/Kathy Willens; pp. 57, 58 © AP/Wide World Photos/ Ana Elisa Fuentes; p.62 © AP/Wide World Photos/Ric Francis; pp. 68, 70 © AP/Wide World Photos/ Ric Field; p. 74 © AP/Wide World Photos/Jim Mone; pp. 77, 78 © AP/Wide World Photos/ John D. McHugh; p. 82 © AP/Wide World Photos/Denis Poroy; pp. 86, 88 © www.istockphoto/Martin Purmensky; p. 91 © Louis Moses/zefa/Corbis; pp. 94, 98 © Holger Winkler/zefa/Corbis; p. 96 © Keith Bedford/Reuters/Corbis; pp. 102, 104 © Rosen Publishing; pp. 110, 115 © Bill Varie/Corbis; p. 112 © Jeff Greenberg/The Image Works; pp. 118, 123 © Helen King/Corbis; p. 120 © www.istockphoto; p.132 © AP/Wide World Photos/ Kevin Wolf.

Design: Evelyn Horovicz; Editor: Joann Jovinelly